P9-DUI-850

HEALING
SOCIETY

ALSO BY DR. SEUNG HEUN LEE

*Brain Respiration: A Powerful Technique
to Energize Your Brain*

Dahn Meditation and Exercise

HEALING SOCIETY

A Prescription for Global Enlightenment

Dr. SEUNG HEUN LEE

WALSCH
W
BOOKS

an imprint of
HAMPTON ROADS
PUBLISHING COMPANY, INC.
www.hrpub.com

Copyright © 2000
by Dr. Seung Heun Lee
All rights reserved, including the right to reproduce this work in any form
whatsoever, without permission in writing from the publisher, except for
brief passages in connection with a review.

Cover design by Marjoram Productions
Cover photo and art by Marjoram Productions
For information write:

Hampton Roads Publishing Company, Inc.
1125 Stoney Ridge Road
Charlottesville, VA 22902

Or call: 804-296-2772
Fax: 804-296-5096
e-mail: hrpc@hrpub.com
Web site: www.hrpub.com

If you are unable to order this book from your local bookseller, you may
order directly from the publisher. Call 1-800-766-8009, toll-free.

Library of Congress Catalog Card Number: 00-110245
ISBN 1-57174-189-5
10 9 8 7 6 5 4 3 2
Printed on acid-free paper in the Canada

Contents

Group Enlightenment—New Human Society

Human Enlightenment— A Spiritual-Cultural Movement

Index

Prayer of Peace

Grand Master Lee's prayer at the opening ceremony in the General Assembly of the United Nations on August 28, 2000:

It is an honor for me to have this opportunity to offer this prayer of peace in front of so many illustrious religious and spiritual leaders. And I am very grateful. Let us pray.

I offer this prayer of peace
Not to any one god nor to many gods
Not to the Christian god
Nor to the Jewish god
Nor the Buddhist god
Nor the Islamic god
And not even to the indigenous gods of many
    nations
But to the divinity within that we all hold inside
That makes us all brothers and sisters
To make us truly a One Family
In the name of humanity.

I offer this prayer of peace
To the cosmic Oneness that is our birthright
And our privilege
And our strength

That should we let it shine and show us the way
Will guide us to the road of peace
Not the Christian peace
Not the Jewish peace
Not the Islamic peace
Nor the Buddhist peace
And not even the indigenous peace of many nations
But the human peace
That has a place in the hearts of all people
To allow us to truly fulfill our divine potential
To become the children of one humanity.

I offer this prayer of peace
To allow us all to realize
The truth of our existence
To allow us all to discover
The sanctity of our lives
To allow us all to seek
The spirituality of our beings
Please allow us to experience
With all our hearts and our souls
The intimate connection to the divine
That we all possess inside
For our bodies are the temples of worship
And our souls the altars
Upon which we shall stand tall
And live out the true meaning
Of our existence.

I offer this prayer of peace
To declare a revolution
Of the human spirit
I wish to announce that
It is now time
For all of us to spiritually awaken
And become enlightened

For the time for the enlightened few is over
The age of elitist enlightenment has passed
For how long do you seek to wait for prophets
To come down from mountaintops
And tell us what to do
We all must become enlightened
To recognize our divinity
To raise up our consciousness
And proclaim our independence
From blind reliance on long ago sages
And find the answers from our own well
Of spiritual wisdom
We must ourselves become the enlightened ones
We must ourselves realize our Oneness
I declare that we must all become "earthlings"
Of the earth
And not of any religion, nation, or race.
But of this earth, for this earth, and by this earth
To create a lasting peace
On earth.

I offer this prayer of peace
For the United Nations
In which we stand here today
To lift itself from the quicksand of politickery
And live out its distinctly spiritual goal
To eradicate the disease of war
And create an equitable and peaceful world.
Let us hope that the UN finds the strength and the
    will
To become the spokesman for all people of the earth
And not just for the few privileged nations
Let us wish upon the UN the wisdom
To become the beacon that we can all follow
To the promised land of love and peace
I pray to thee

God of all gods, the divine that lives within us and
    connects us in One Life
That you grant us the vision
To establish a Spiritual UN
That will guide us into the next millennium.

I offer this prayer of peace
With all my fellow "earthlings"
For a lasting peace on earth.

Preface:
The True Purpose of Life

I was alone in a remote mountain, having gone without food or sleep for twenty-one days. I was at my utmost limit, in body and mind. I had an excruciatingly painful headache that pierced through my head in rhythmic and dreadful pounding. My body wouldn't move, nor my tongue form a word. And it was at this moment that the cosmos opened up inside me and swept me into her arms with a loud resounding moment of enlightenment, a deafening crash that seemed to transport me to another world. "Cosmic Mind is My Mind and Cosmic Energy is My Energy!" my mouth automatically croaked in eternal joy, voicing the Oneness that I had glimpsed before and had even known intellectually, but had never felt at this level of profound depth.

This voice told me that my body is not me, but mine. It told me that my mind is not me, but mine. It assured me that the Cosmic Mind is my mind and that the Cosmic Energy is my energy. Through this moment, I came to feel the all-encompassing rhythm of life. I experienced the light, the sound, and the vibration that formed the source of all life, absorbing and understanding in wonder the Cosmic Order within that governed all things. Through that moment, I had found my True Self, after so many years of fruitless search.

I was born in Korea in midst of chaos and change.

It was 1950. On June 25 of that year, the Soviet-trained and -equipped armies of North Korea invaded the woefully unprepared South Korea all along the Thirty-eighth Parallel, an imaginary line along an expanse of lush greenery marked by an unending stretch of razor-sharp wire fence that divided North from South Korea, forcibly separating families, friends, and lovers. The North Koreans sought to unify the whole Korean Peninsula and free us from the evil American imperialists, and the South Koreans resisted the insidious encroachment of the Stalinist communist dictatorship with equal fervor. Both claimed to be the true inheritors of the new Korea, after the long and torturous Japanese occupation. For the next three years, the forces of socialism and capitalism came together with a cataclysmic effect on the Korean continent with all the power and fanaticism of young ideologies, eventually involving more than sixteen countries and marking the beginning of the Cold War. At the end, the war would claim more than four million lives on both sides, including those of more than fifty thousand American GIs.

To the Koreans, the war was a brutal, yet eye-opening, introduction to the world at large. We saw that there existed in the world all different types of people: whites, blacks, Indians, large, small, and dark. We were introduced to different ideas and ways of living, acting, laughing, and crying. We saw that people spoke different tongues, mind-boggling in all their variety and complexities. It was a world of stark contrasts, immediate fear of death and constant struggle for life, grief-stricken chant over a lost son and bright laughter at the sight of a returning daughter, the sight of corpses littering the streets and cries of newborns amidst the rubble.

It was in this world that I grew up, asking questions about life and death as early as I can remember, questions that were eventually answered in that one spectacular moment of enlightenment after countless years of all-consuming search. And I write this book now because I want to call upon the world to embark on an Enlightenment Revolution, a massive spiritual awakening that will sweep across the Earth with a thundering speed, bringing the joy of enlightenment to everyone. I write this book now to let everyone know of their own right to enlightenment, that enlightenment is not only the realm of the saintly, and that the massive enlightenment of humanity is the only lasting solution to our real problems.

My own journey started when I was five years old and felt, for the first time, the mysterious and warm power of *Ki* energy, the force that animates all life and fills the cosmos itself. More popularized by the Chinese pronunciation of *Chi* in the West, *Ki* is the invisible energy that goes around and through all things, acting as the invisible yarn from which everything in this universe is woven. Through my personal explorations of *Ki* energy, I was able to reach a high level of energy control, allowing me to perform some so-called miraculous feats, such as communing with spirits, curing incurable diseases, helping paralyzed people walk, and calming mentally unstable people. This control is not as fantastic as it may seem at first glance, for all it involves is training and technique. It is akin to training to be an athlete. The road may be difficult and long, but definitely doable with enough determination and talent. You don't need to be specially chosen by God; you just need to choose to do it yourself. There is nothing spiritual or holy about performing these feats of energy, although it can act as a method through which you can reach into your divine spirituality and attain enlightenment. I will speak more of this later.

However, no matter how high my level of energy control reached, I realized the limits of creating such energy phenomena, for it remained just another technique or skill, no different from playing tennis or singing a song well. Just because you can communicate with invisible spirits doesn't mean that you know the answer to life's ultimate purpose. Just because you can draw in and send forth energy doesn't mean that you can satisfy the questions that lie buried deep down in your soul. You need to be spiritually awakened to have those answers. It was this realization that led me to more search, finally culminating in that deafening moment of liberation that I described in the beginning.

The purpose of life is really no big deal, although people have generally viewed the question, Why am I here? as the ultimate in self-exploration. As with any question, when you look at it from a different point of view, it is very simple. When you accept that human beings are spiritual beings and that our physical and mental selves, including our personalities, are just tools that we are given to affect our spiritual nature, then the answer just presents itself. The true purpose of life lies in the spiritual maturing process of individuals, society, and humanity as a whole. We are here on Earth in such and such shape, form, and mind to strive for the completion of our spiritual selves, not only as individuals but as the whole of humanity. We are here to heal our souls and come closer to recovering the divine nature—our spiritual nature— through the physical and mental tools that we have been given. "My body is mine, not me." "My mind is mine, not me." These two sentences form the centerpiece of this spiritual point of view. If the physical body and mental acuity that you have been born with are not *you,* but just tools temporarily lent you for you to experience things that will mature you spiritually, then who is the real you? Simple. Your spiritual nature. And since your spiritual nature is essentially a part of the Cosmic Spirit, and so is the spiritual nature of everyone else's, then your spiritual nature and someone else's spiritual nature are parts of the same Grand Spirit. This is why every spiritual and religious leader in the history of humankind has told us that we are One. Another way to describe the spiritually maturing process, this spiritual awakening that is our true purpose of life, is enlightenment. The true purpose of life for every human being is, therefore, to reach enlightenment.

I found the way to express my true purpose in this lifetime. It is to educate people so that they too may experience the spiritual awakening, the enlightenment, that I have experienced. It was to educate people to open their eyes to their own spirituality. It was to make people realize that enlightenment was an inherent right and the norm, not the rare exception. To do this, I realized that people needed to recover their physical and energy balance first, before delving into their spiritual search. Therefore, I utilized the energy-sensitizing and controlling techniques I learned during my long training process before achieving spiritual awakening. From the various exercises, meditation, and martial arts that I practiced, I devised the most effective method of simple exercises designed to allow people to start on their road to physical, mental, and spiritual health. I called this *"Dahn Hak."* I systematized this *Dahn Hak* technique, which consists of simple stretching, calisthenics, breathing techniques, and meditation, and sought to teach it to others to help them regain their health and balance. I started this in a public park, with one student, a victim of partial paralysis from a stroke.

Although *Dahn Hak* starts out as a physical exercise, its true purpose lies in helping the individual recover his physical health and ethical foundation on his way to becoming a "spiritual" person who is nonetheless successful in the everyday world. At the same time, *Dahn Hak* aims at the spiritual enlightenment not only of the individual but of the whole society and of humanity, for individual and group enlightenment are different sides of the same coin. They cannot be separated.

In fifteen years, this *Dahn Hak* exercise has grown to include more than one million members in over three hundred centers in South Korea alone, and close to one hundred thousand members in over fifty centers in the United States, including a meditation retreat center in Sedona, Arizona, and a holistic health club in Closter, New Jersey. It has become a huge success, way beyond my initial dreams, because *Dahn Hak* gained a reputation for helping people to recover their health and balance in a simple, easy, and effective way. It has become an exercise trend, the choice among holistic exercises, for its eye-opening effectiveness in helping people recover their lost physical and energy balance. Then it is the individual's choice to explore further into their spirituality. It is a private choice that each one of us has to make. Nothing can be forced. And it is my sincere hope that *Dahn Hak* can help lead people on their path to spiritual health when they do make the choice, not as an alternative to their respective faith traditions, but as a mean to help them become better Christians, Buddhists, or Muslims.

I have also fine-tuned *Dahn Hak* to develop a technique called "Brain Respiration," through which you can literally use your brainpower to awaken your dormant spirituality. Brain Respiration strips away the mysticism from enlightenment and makes it an everyday reality for all. Brain Respiration lays the physiological foundation to this phenomenon called "enlightenment."

That is what I ultimately want, for people to recover their hidden spirituality, and I want to make it as easy as possible for them. For that is my life's goal, to help people recover their inherent right to enlightenment. For that is what this world needs, a collective Enlightenment Revolution to sweep across the face of this Earth, allowing humanity to go beyond its current problems into a higher spiritual plane.

For that I write this book.

Seung Heun Lee
Sedona, Arizona
January 2000

Introduction:
Time to Greet the Dawn

The dawn of the new millennium is here.

However, no matter how close or bright that first light is, you cannot see it unless you are awake. Unless you open your eyes, light will still remain darkness to you. The beauty of dawn can be appreciated only by those who are awake to greet the dawn.

It is time for us to open our eyes. It is time for us to awaken to new possibilities and make them real. It is time for us to awaken our dormant spirituality—first as individuals, then as whole nations, and finally as the whole of humanity—and raise up our collective consciousness.

Poised at the dawning of the new millennium, we are still faced with the brutality of the civil war in Albania, the unspeakable cruelty of the fights between the Hutus and Tutsis in Africa, the stubborn hatred exhibited in the cruel battles between Russians and Chechens, and the insidious disease of violence and bigotry tragically illustrated by the twelve separate multiple shootings in the United States in 1999 alone. All these and other events that create headlines around the world today only go to show that we are still surrounded by confusion and darkness.

In order to defeat this darkness, we need an enlightened society. This society will come about not because one or two individuals have been somehow blessed with enlightenment. This society will come about when this enlightenment has become a worldwide phenomenon, when the possibility and the actuality of collective enlightenment have become accepted by humanity. Enlightenment must become a social movement that sweeps across the face of the Earth.

What is enlightenment? Enlightenment means listening to the True Self that lies within. Like a butterfly within a withered cocoon, everyone has a wellspring of beautiful divinity inside. Belief in this divinity will imbue life itself with the wonderful aroma of peace and harmony. Everyone is like a flower, uniquely beautiful in full bloom, no matter what type or color or shape. When you meet this True Self, you will experience an absolute happiness. It won't be the relative happiness that comes from being richer or better-looking than others, but rather, the absolute happiness that comes from within, not bound by the needs and desires of the small "me-self." It will be the absolute happiness that comes from the absolute knowledge that everything and everyone is One. It will be a knowledge that you will have personally and profoundly experienced.

Enlightenment means True Love, the thing that makes us truly human and sets us above the other animals that share this earth with us. Without knowing our True Self, we cannot know True Love. True Love is not selfish love, egotistical love, controlling love, or domineering love. True Love is love that is all-encompassing and willingly given regardless of its recipients. True Love is the love we hold for Heaven, Earth, Man, and all of existence. Why do we have to seek enlightenment? To recover True Love in our hearts. By losing the memory of True Love in our hearts, we have fallen from being gods to being animals. Now we need to rejoin the ranks of the divine.

Notwithstanding all the wonderful rhetoric about True Love and True Self, however, enlightenment is not sweet-sounding words and abstract concepts. Enlightenment is a concrete, reality-based goal that everyone can attain. Enlightenment is also a physiological phenomenon that you can achieve using your brain. Enlightenment can happen in the everyday world. Not as a freak of accident, but as the result of a series of concrete steps that can be accomplished through will, discipline, and a sense of responsibility, like any other worthwhile goal. Enlightenment just happens to be the most worthwhile goal that I can imagine for a human being. The possibility of the universality of enlightenment—this is exactly what I want to emphasize in this book.

Enlightenment is a two-step process.

First, enlightenment is a choice. Enlightenment is not a sudden realization accompanied by some lightning and thunder after forty days of fasting prayer. The difficulties and hard training that I went through were because of ignorance and stupidity, not to be a model for the rest of the world to follow. The thunder and lightning are an expression of exasperation on the part of the Cosmic Mind to tell you that you are already enlightened. You just have to live up to it. My true enlightenment was realizing that I had been enlightened all this time. Enlightenment is a simple choice that you make to live your life for the betterment and benefit of all those around you. The question is, how do we know how to be beneficial to others? But the answer we already have! We all know how to be beneficial. We all know how to be loving and caring to others. We all have this inherent goodness in us. You cannot deny this. Enlightenment is just the choice to accept this goodness, your True Self and to actualize it through True Love. In concrete terms and actions, not just as an escapist emotional high that will soon disappear.

Second, enlightenment is the discipline that you need to live out your choice. The discipline to face the opposition and derision from various cynics and still stay the course. The discipline to conquer your lesser desires and live out your choice to build a truly worthwhile existence. The discipline to train and keep up your spiritual fitness. This is enlightenment. Enlightenment is choice and discipline. Enlightenment is action. Enlightenment is reality.

The twenty-first century will be the Age of Spirituality. We cannot deny that materialism has failed to bring us genuine and lasting happiness. Political and economic institutions have become diseased. Politics cannot cure politics. Economy cannot save economy. We may have achieved a breakthrough in material science, but we have not advanced far enough in spiritual science. We are currently not spiritually mature enough to handle the material advances we have made.

Now we need to devote as much effort in advancing spiritual science as we have devoted to material science. We need to evolve and mature spiritually. We human beings still cannot solve our biggest problems without war or violence. We still do not know how to love unconditionally. Neither our mentality nor our spirituality has significantly advanced in the thousands of years since the beginning of recorded history.

The Renaissance came about when the ancient teachings of Greece and Rome burst upon the Dark Ages like a brilliant ray of light. Today, we already have the teachings to effect a similarly grand spiritual renaissance in the world. In the spiritual traditions of Korea, we encounter the philosophy of *Chun-Ji-In,* which teaches us that the Heaven-Earth-human triumvirate is One; the concept of *Hong-Ik Ingan* and *E-wha Saegae,* which places the utmost worth of a person in his or her service to others; and the movement of *Yuln'yo* culture, which allows one to learn the concept of universal harmony in his or her everyday life. I will be introducing these terms and concepts from my tradition throughout the book. But you probably know these concepts already, just by other names, for these ideas and teachings are integral parts of many cultures and spiritual traditions. And how are these concepts different from Jesus' love or Buddha's mercy or Confucius' ethics? They are not, for we, all of humanity, have a shared spiritual heritage. And this is only natural because we all have come from One. One Awareness. One Energy.

By learning about and spreading such a treasure-trove of spiritual heritage throughout the globe, we may finally produce a worldwide Spiritual-Cultural Movement that surpasses and encompasses the varied religions, governments, and economies around the world. Only through such a movement can we produce a cure for what ails the individual, the nation, and humanity. The problems we face now cannot be solved in parts only. They require a comprehensive solution. What is needed is an Enlightenment Revolution.

To make enlightenment an everyday and worldwide reality, we need three separate yet related phases: the enlightenment of the individual, the enlightenment of the group, and the enlightenment of all of humanity.

The first will be accomplished with Brain Respiration, through which the individual will learn how to get in touch with the Creator Within and access the highest Truth, riding on a stream of his or her own energy into a higher awareness. The second will be accomplished through a culture of New Human Society, in which enlightened individuals join together in harmony to help others reach the Creator Within and share their enlightenment with as many as possible. "New Human" is just another word for *"Hong-Ik Ingan,"* the traditional Korean term for someone who lives for the betterment of all. The third will be accomplished via a worldwide Spiritual-Cultural Movement that sweeps the Earth in a blaze of harmony and cooperation, led by those New Humans who have made enlightenment a natural and obvious part of our society. The underlying principles of this movement lie in harmony and cooperation and coexistence. Harmony is the most beautiful flower that blossoms out of a society.

For how long are we going to continue to learn only? For how long are we just going to study the Truths spoken by Jesus, Buddha, and other Wise Teachers? Now it is time to live out this Truth. We all need to discover the light of divinity that we possess inside and then let this light illuminate the road that we take. A lone superhero is no longer enough to carry all our hopes. Our hopes can only be carried by the multitude who accept and let this light of divinity blossom forth from their collective hearts. When you open your mind, it can cover the universe. When you close your mind, it will become smaller than the smallest pinprick.

I declare that it is time to open up our minds and greet the dawn. I declare that it is time for an Enlightenment Revolution to forever cure the ills of our society. I declare that it is time for a Spiritual-Cultural Movement to uplift the whole of humanity to its spiritual heritage. And if enough people join in and open up their minds and reach for their divine potential within . . .

Ah, let us all imagine the wonderful possibilities.

Can you imagine a world in which the highest value is placed upon the creation of harmony and cooperation? Can you not imagine a society in which the highest goals would be to seek the fulfillment and completion of your souls? A place in which spiritual goals are placed higher on the totem pole than how much money you earn? Is such a place possible?

More than possible. It has to be created. It is not an option.

History is filled with amazing twists and turns. Until the Middle Ages, humankind was mired in the fearsome world of the arbitrary God who was the center of their universe. Starting with the Renaissance, humans developed the intellectual skills and courage to break out of this suffocating divine dictatorship and start the road on which reason reigned supreme. And this road has led us to the present, the Age of Materialism, in which Man is king.

Materialism has provided us with myriad creature comforts and benefits, for who would have thought that we could land on Mars and fly to the ends of the Earth in a few hours? All these advances in such a short time! Yet, it has cost us dearly in terms of our collective humanity. Personal egotism and group centrism, a form of tribalism, constantly fed through our unending competition, have robbed us of our true nature and created a framework of fear and anxiety in which to live. One doesn't have to be a prophet to see that we will self-destruct if we stay on this road.

Incredible advances in technology have been made possible by the forces of democracy and capitalism, this everyone knows. Democracy has made great strides in expanding personal freedom and the ability to use talents. Capitalism has created a worldwide stage on which to showcase our talents and be rewarded for them. But we enjoy the technological luxuries today at the cost of making constant competition the sole arbitrator of success, with its brutal efficiency and merciless execution. Competition has led us into constant anxiety about our very existence, deepening our self-destructive need for security, recognition, and domination. Overwhelmed by these destructive needs, we have lost touch with that which makes us human: True Love. We have ignored our True Self. We have forgotten the divinity within.

Now it's time for another amazing turn in the history of humankind.

Just as we broke free from the stifling grip of an arbitrary God, we need to break out of the equally smothering grip of materialism, creating a society based on genuine harmony, in which God and humans join together to implement a truly universal view of existence. God and humans will coexist as equal rulers of a world in which the ingenuity of humans is guided by the gentle love of God, where the sharp logic of humans is tempered by the compassion of God, and where the loud clamor of competition is drowned out by the soothing rhythm of our spirituality.

To cure social ills, to overcome the insidious domination of materialism, to usher in a new era of spiritualism, and to create a lasting world peace based on trust and harmony—these are the goals toward which I have devoted my life. It is for these aims that I have developed and introduced *Dahn Hak* and Brain Respiration as ways in which ordinary people can reach a state of enlightenment. It is for these ideals that thousands of fellow spiritual compatriots, past and present, have devoted their lives. It is for these goals that we should now devote our lives to creating a deliriously happy spiritual playground in which we can have a jolly old time. For the secret of life ultimately lies in just having fun together.

Individual enlightenment. Group enlightenment. Human enlightenment.

Brain Respiration. New Human Society. Spiritual-Cultural Movement.

Let us all join hands and have fun together.

Enlightenment—
Yuln'yo

Enlightenment as True Self

Your heart is the Heaven. It is the space itself. It is time. Inside your heart lies the cosmos. You are the eternal Heaven. You are an insignificant space dust. You can exist as the smallest life-form while simultaneously encompassing the whole Heaven without beginning or end, limitless space, and eternal time. You are all these and more.

When you go to a Buddhist temple in the Orient, you will see a series of pictures of a farmer leading a cow. In the first frame, there is only a calf running around in the fields, stepping on the crops and wreaking general havoc. The second frame has the now-grown calf with a nose ring and getting a spanking from the farmer for misbehaving. The third frame has the farmer leading the cow slowly down a path, guiding it left and right. The fourth frame has the farmer riding the cow, directing it with the playing of a flute. In the fifth frame, the cow is gone, and only the farmer is left.

The cow represents your greed, needs, and appetites. The farmer represents your True Self—who you truly are beneath all these shells of personality, emotions, fear, and everything else that has been weighing you down. At first, we mistake that the cow is our True Self. That is, we only consist of the sum of our needs, appetites, and greed. Basically, we are what we want, without any deeper considerations. At this level, we are like animals. We eat when we want, we sleep when we want, we urinate and excrete wherever we feel like it, and have sex when the desire comes over us. Just because we surround ourselves with modern conveniences and some social affectations doesn't mean that we are spiritually any better than a dog or a cow. At this level, we are happy when our needs are fulfilled, and we are unhappy when they are not. At this level, we have no doubts, no questions about life itself. At this level, you have completely lost touch with your True Self. You are just like that calf running amok among the crops, creating paths of destruction without care or knowledge.

Then the farmer places a ring through your nose, a painful process but a necessary one to teach you where you need to go. He tugs you here and there with a rope, teaching you the things that you can do and places that you can go and taps you with a stick to gently keep you awake. As you go through this stage, you slowly realize that there are easier ways to get to where you want to be. More importantly, you are discovering how to get there.

Once you pass this stage, the farmer (your True Self) can direct you by his voice alone, without having to pull on the rope. You have developed a mechanism to control your greed and appetites. You feel the old urges, but you know how to control them without needing someone else's help.

Soon, the farmer can direct you without even a word. He just plays his flute as he rides along, and you know where to go automatically. It is at this stage that you can see the farmer clearly and the farmer sees you. There is harmony to the relationship. Your ego-self recognizes your True Self.

In the last stage, there is no cow. Only the farmer is left. Only your True Self stands alone, because you have learned to shed your layers of greed and appetites. At this point, there is no need for a cow (your ego). Your own feet can carry you to wherever you wish.

Which of the two do you have more of in you? The cow or the farmer? In many of us, the cow is stronger and is dragging the farmer around, wandering all over the field, lost, and without a specific destination. It is only when you let the farmer take hand and direct the cow that you will find yourself on the right path, because your True Self knows where it wants to go.

Why do you feel anxious and fearful? Why do you feel a tearing of your emotions? It is because you are letting the cow lead the farmer.

Your True Self is the light, the beacon by which you should guide your life. You have to let it shine. Otherwise, you are living in darkness, wandering helplessly among the fears and anxieties that surround us. In the darkness, even the fleeting light of the firefly looks bright. And you spend all your energies chasing after these lights, not even realizing that a far greater light lies inside you. Don't throw away your life chasing after an insect that will blink out and die soon after you catch it. Don't spend all your time chasing after a momentary high. The single biggest source of health and happiness lies within your True Self. If you search within your True Self, you will find absolute health and everlasting happiness. If you search within your petty needs and greed, you will wander the darkness forever. Without lighting up your True Self, you won't find out what health and happiness truly mean.

Our history is one of struggle and conflict rising out of the need for power and strength. It is a history of hate and animosity. This happened because we didn't let the farmer in us take over and lead us on to the path. If you don't allow your True Self to shine through, you will always live in the midst of fear and darkness, in effect, allowing yourself to run around in the fields when the path was right there in front of you. And in darkness, you fall into the trap of self-serving emotions, egotism, and complexes. Within this trap, it is impossible to develop understanding and sense of cooperation.

Hate has been building up for decades, centuries, and millennia, and we do not know when this will explode. It has almost been our birthright to inherit the hates and prejudices

5

that our ancestors held. This is the Original Sin. In the Bible, there are Cain and Abel. Who did Cain kill? His brother, Abel. They say all human beings descended from Cain. They say we have the blood of a murderer coursing through our veins. But we also have the blood of the saints running through our veins. We have the blood of the countless enlightened ones, whether they are known or not, intermixing with Cain's blood and giving us life.

If someone thinks of himself as possessing only the blood of Cain, does this person have hope or not? Of course not. If you think you are the bad seed, what kind of motivation do you have to put yourself on the right path? Only when you start believing that you have the blood of Jesus, the Buddha, Moses, and all the other prophets and saints in you can you start believing in the possibility of your own goodness. And at the moment of belief, you will feel the blood of pure goodness course through you like some live electrical wire, slowly gaining in strength. Only with belief in your goodness can you start being good, begin finding your True Self.

So, it's a choice you have to make. Whose blood will you let run through your veins? Cain's or Jesus'? Cain's or the Buddha's? Cain's or the prophets'? Ultimately, this is your blood, your choice. Make the right choice. Make the choice that will lead you to your True Self.

We talk a lot about the soul. Every human being has a soul. Your soul is in your heart, pure and active. A ruthless mugger who has robbed hundreds of people can still feel a momentary pang as he walks by a crippled old beggar rustling through a garbage can. A multiple murderer can still have feelings for the suffering of a child with cancer. Even the worst of us still have that gem of purity and love.

When a sudden desire to help somebody pops into your head without calculation or expectation, it's your soul talking. All of us have had this experience. Your soul is always talking to you. But there are people who listen to that voice and then there are those who think, "Hey, I've got my own problems!"

and drown out the beautiful sound with their own little human noises. Even now, when you really want to hear your soul speaking, you can. And when you hear it, you grab on to it and never let it go silent. Make that sound grow larger in volume until it drowns out all the petty cacophony in your life with a loud, beautiful symphony.

To listen to your soul is to lighten up your True Self. The root of your soul lies in your True Self. And where does the root of your True Self lie? In the Cosmic Oneness of which we are all a part. When you let your True Self shine through, you naturally realize that you and I are one. Only through this realization can we really come together as a society, as a people, and as a humanity. Only then can we become One. By realizing that we are already One.

Try coming to this understanding through politics and ideologies. Not in a thousand years will you come to a lasting understanding or peace. Imagine you and your friend want to make up after a huge fight. If you weigh the pros and cons of this makeup, if you judge whether you won or lost, if you have even a modicum of thought in your mind that you are making up because you might want something from your friend later and don't want to antagonize him, will that lead to a true makeup? Of course not. When you want to make peace or make up your differences, you can't do it through the process of cold calculations. If you are weighing the advantages of making peace against the disadvantages, that means that you are not even remotely ready to make peace. If you want to make peace, make peace. Don't make peace with prerequisites or conditions. There is no such thing as conditional peace. Or conditional forgiveness. The important thing is to share your heart. If you really think the other person is worthy enough to make peace with, then show the proper respect and don't start calculating the pros and cons. Start forgiving and making peace. Start listening to your heart and soul.

Only when we light up our True Selves can we create a truly harmonious society. Close your eyes and look at your inner self. Gaze and observe. Perhaps you have so far been more aware of your outer surroundings than your inner state. If you truly want to change, you have to stop caring about other people's eyes and judgments. If you don't, you will end up living only according to what others think of you. If you really want to change, you have to listen to your soul.

Right now, it may be difficult for you to listen because you are on another frequency. The soul may be screaming, but you can't hear because you are on the wrong channel. The sound of your soul is muffled because of all the garbage and dirt on top. Then, how do we clean off the dirt and the garbage? By cleaning and clearing frequently and as hard as we can. Day and night. Day and night. Because if you let the dirt stay on too long, it will solidify and become part of you. It will become your flesh. And when you want to get rid of it then, it will hurt, it will bleed, and it will make you scream. But this is what you have to do. You have to look at yourself and pour the boiling water of your soul upon yourself to clean out all the dirt that has piled up. What will be left over, like a diamond in the rough, will be your True Self. If you really want to change for the better, you may have to be strong enough to cut off your own flesh to get rid of the dirt on top. As Jesus taught, "If your right hand offends you, cut it off and throw it away."

In the Korean tradition, in order to learn from a Wise Teacher, you have to spend three years chopping wood, three years cleaning the house, and three years cooking before the Teacher would even deign to speak to you about anything of import. There is a good reason for this seeming waste of time. It is to help you learn to kill your pride, your sense of judgment, and your sense of worth. Only when you have emptied yourself of all the dirt that you have accumulated from the outside world can you start filling back up with your True Self. You will hurt. You will bleed. You will scream in pain. But you have to clean yourself until you get to that layer that's truly you.

This is not an easy task, to unearth the purity of your soul from underneath all the dirt that you have mistakenly thought was the real you. If you don't have the will, you will give up. This is not a road that someone who is attached to his or her physical self can travel. This is not a fruit that someone who cannot let go of his petty needs can pluck. This is the road to absolute freedom. This is the road to your True Self. You have to give it your utmost love and devotion. You can only arrive at this destination when you truly appreciate its worth. Your True Self is worth more than ten—no, one hundred—stars put together. You have to be willing to give up the Milky Way itself to find your True Self. That's how precious it is. Yet, we would trade the preciousness of our true selves for the excess comfort of an extra TV or a bigger house. What a lousy bargain! Truly a deal with the devil.

Close your eyes and look silently at yourself again. Think back. What have I done today? Whom have I met? Have I committed any deceit? Have I hidden my True Self again? Have I represented myself falsely? Have I been truly honest with myself and with others? When you can answer yes to this last question, you are on your way to cleaning out all the dirt you have so far accumulated. The road to your True Self lies not through logic and calculations, but through choice and discipline—the conscious choice to take that road, and the discipline to stay on it in the face of obstacles. So, sweep off the dirt and the grime that's pretending to be you. Let your True Self shine through.

Repeat the following:

My body is mine, not me.

My mind is mine, not me.

Do not be a slave to either your body or your mind. The true master of you is your True Self. Most of us are trapped behind this mistaken belief that our bodies are us, that our faces, races, ethnic groups, height, girth, aches, and pains are actually us. No. *An emphatic no!* Your body is yours, not you. You are here to utilize the body you happened to be born with

9

in this lifetime for whatever purposes that your True Self has in store for you.

Your body is a precious and useful property, nothing more. When you are done with your current life, you throw it away and move on. Your physical body is not the reason for which you are born, no matter how beautiful or strong. If you live through your life thinking that your body is what you are, you are a slave to the needs and appetites of your body, and will seek to satisfy those until you die. Instead of mastering your body, you will have spent your entire life being mastered *by* your body.

The same goes for your mind. This is even more insidious. Even those of us who are aware that our bodies are not truly us, often mistakenly believe that our minds are what we truly are. *Wrong!* Your personality, your knowledge, your wisdom, your emotional makeup, your thoughts, your method of deduction and induction, all these are not who you truly are. You are not a quick-tempered Latino male with a penchant for computer programming who enjoys football games on weekends and good detective stories. You are not a patient, virtuous woman who has good judgment and shrewd mind when it comes to "too good to be true" offers. These characteristics are not you. You are not here on this Earth in human form to be some kind of a cosmic newspaper personal ad. Do not reduce yourself to what your body and mind consist of. You are far greater than that. You are eternal. You are infinite. Your True Self is the cosmos itself. Don't ever fall into the trap of thinking that you are your physical and mental self. You have a higher spiritual existence—your True Self. Your current physical and mental manifestations are here only to serve the purpose of your spiritual master, your True Self, as part of a healing and completing process of cosmic harmony and balance. Do not sell yourself short.

When you let your True Self guide you, you are letting Jesus or Buddha himself guide your life. You are letting God be your personal guide, because all of us have the divine inside us.

When you feel your True Self, you will first feel an appreciation for everything around you. You will appreciate that you are able to open your eyes every morning. You will appreciate the intake of every breath. You will be thankful for movements in your arms and legs. And when you are thankful, you become diligent. You do not waste time, and you work hard because you are so thankful for everything that you have. Then you become harmonious. You get along with everyone. You think of others first. You do the hardest work first, you are always thankful, you are always forgiving. And if everyone is thankful, diligent, and harmonious, then we have a genuine Heaven on Earth. This is what we call *"Hong-Ik Ingan, E-wha Saegae,"* in the Korean tradition. Directly translated, "Wide-Benefits Human, Everything-Harmonious World." This kind of world will not be the offspring of some political or religious theory. This world will spring out of a mass spiritual revolution that allows people to get in touch with their true selves.

Enlightenment means listening to your True Self.

Enlightenment as True Love

What is enlightenment? As I said before, enlightenment is finding your True Self and making it work through you. It is doing the will of your True Self.

First, you have to make the choice to want to be enlightened. You have to make up your mind to open up your eyes and ears and grab the chance when it is offered to you. If you are not sure about wanting enlightenment, then all the good and righteous words in the world will not make a difference.

Enlightenment is the discipline to follow the road to finding your True Self, amidst all the distractions. What distractions? The distractions of all the dirt and garbage that you have picked up, covering your True Self.

Enlightenment is achieved through action. There is no one as foolish as the person who waits passively for some bolt of enlightenment to come down from the sky. "Someday I will be awakened to the Truth." What a foolish idea. The passage of time guarantees nothing except that your physical body will wear out.

Imagine that you have an itch in your foot. There could be many causes of such an itch. So you go to a doctor and he says that it's athlete's foot. Now you know the cause. But just because you know the reason doesn't mean it won't itch anymore. It still itches. So, what do you do? You take an antifungal spray or lotion and put in on the affected areas until you are cured. Just once? Of course not. As often as it takes to get rid of the itch. This is the same process that you would go through to be enlightened. You ask the questions, you find the way to the answer, and you work at it until you grasp the answer. This is how enlightenment comes.

Then, what are the questions that one needs to ask. Why was I born, where do I come from, and where am I going? The same questions that humankind has been asking for millennia. Like an itch that won't go away. If you know the answers to these questions, then you are enlightened.

And how do you find the answers? Just get in touch with your True Self. All that remains is that you work at it until you make that connection with who you truly are. This will require courage, dedication, and discipline. You will sweat, you will feel a wrenching pain, and you will hurt. But once you make the journey, you will realize that all the pain was unnecessary, because everything that was causing you this pain was an illusion. Made-up. It will be like building yourself up to jump into a pool of freezing water only to realize afterwards that it is the most luxurious, warm, and soothing bath that you have ever experienced. You will laugh that you ever had any apprehension at all. But before you make that jump, the apprehension you feel is very real. Enlightenment is an exercise in trust.

Have you ever been stuck in traffic that won't move an inch for an hour? Have you then noticed how some people deal with the time? Some sing out loud, moving their heads to and fro as if they were the original artists, rocking the whole car on its chassis. Some people honk for a minute at a time, as if the car in front of them was somehow the reason for clogging up the whole city block. Others even break out a deck of cards to whittle away the time while stuck in traffic. What do all these activities tell us? That people need to be constantly in motion. That they get nervous with time during which they don't do anything. That they are ever so anxious to get on with something, anything.

"Time is money" is the motto on which everything runs. After all, there are always others who will be spending their time constructively while you are stuck in traffic. You will be falling behind. Somebody else will take over your job, your security, your family, your everything, and you will lose if you waste any more time in this damned traffic. You will *lose the game.*

From where does this anxiety come? Where else—our competitive social paradigm. We think that in order to survive, we have to be better than everyone else. Our fear of losing is what drives us. We have forgotten that we are all interconnected, not just with each other, but with the whole cosmos, and that what affects one part affects every other part. We have forgotten what our True Selves know.

In the midst of this almost instinctive anxiety, human beings are nevertheless looking to escape it. We somehow know that there is something better than all this constant instability. That's why we try to explain away our anxiety with logic, conquer it with religion, legislate it with government, and soothe it away with therapy, only to fail. Yet, we have to somehow appease this gnawing anxiety that we feel. So we seek a form of fleeting security through competition, for by beating others we create a sense of superiority and security in knowing that we are at least less anxious or fearful than that person. Then we become addicted to this momentary high and make it our life's goal. How much we make, how many cars we have, what wonderful vacations we will go to next . . . beat the Joneses, or at least keep up with them. And because of this instinctive anxiousness, we hurt each other, becoming the reasons for all the bad memories of others, and all the bad information about this world that is passed on to others. Only a person truly at peace with who he or she is can be loving and magnanimous. If we are forever anxious and nervous about something, we can't afford to be generous. We have to take the next person down to move on up in this world, even if we have to step on that person's broken back. We have to look out for number one.

Those who seek enlightenment need to be simple. You can't have complicated thoughts in your mind if you want a spiritual awakening. It's like finding a needle in the middle of a muddy pool of water. If you stick your hand in the pool and stir up all the mud, how will you be able to find it? You need to let the mud settle to the bottom and the water to clear before you can see the needle. Then you can reach in and gently but firmly grab on to it. Enlightenment requires a simple belief. Simple choice. Simple courage. Simple discipline. Simple action.

The next big question: why seek enlightenment? Once you are enlightened, then what? Is there anything further? Oh, yes. The reason to seek enlightenment is to recover the True Love that exists in our hearts. Not just to recover it in a passive sense, but to actualize it through concrete actions that benefit those around you. This will make enlightenment an experience, not just a concept.

Many people have been enlightened throughout the history of mankind, not just Jesus, the Buddha, or Muhammad. Thousands of nameless saints, holy men, and seers have realized the Oneness. They realized that everything in physical life is an illusion and that their True Selves lie in higher dimension. But many of them hid themselves from the world at large until they died. Others killed themselves. Why go on living in this illusion? What fun is there after you have seen through the veil of disguise? If you know, truly know, that all the things around you are temporary and illusionary, what could there possibly be on this Earth to keep you here? Therefore, many enlightened ones said good-bye to this world in one form or another, quietly and without making themselves known. It was here that they failed. They failed to love. Truly. They understood enlightenment only as awareness, not as experience.

Some may argue that they allowed themselves to fade away because they realized that it was not yet time for their enlightenment to be actualized or for their teachings to be propagated; that they knew they were born at a time in which the seed of enlightenment could not possibly germinate. And so they disappeared without making themselves known. Maybe so. But such thoughts are fundamentally defeatist. It is wisdom without heart. It is knowledge without courage. It is enlightenment without True Love. What if they could influence just one person in a positive way? What if they could make one flower blossom in the middle of thousands of acres of barren land?

They failed to realize that true enlightenment can be tested only in reality. Enlightenment is something that's fundamentally alive, needing sharpening and honing to reach its sharpest potential. It is not a static state of mind. Many people make the mistake of thinking that enlightenment is something that always looks beyond reality into the realm of the ideal. However, after enlightenment, you need to come back to reality and do your work here to change the things that ought to be changed. This is True Love. True Love means coming back into the masses to proclaim the Truth when you know that you will be crucified for it. True Love requires courage. I believe that one who indulges in his or her own sense of enlightenment but fails to make a positive difference in the lives of others is not truly enlightened. That someone has failed to truly love, either through a lack of courage or a preponderance of egotism.

Enlightenment that ends with the individual is not genuine enlightenment. Enlightenment that has not been tested through battles in reality is not true enlightenment. Enlightenment that has not made a difference in the world is not true enlightenment. Only when enlightenment is used for the betterment of all humankind is it truly a great enlightenment. And such an enlightenment can be achieved only by actively recovering and cultivating your sense of True Love for all of existence.

I visited Nepal a few years back and happened to attend a crowning ceremony of a three-year-old who was reputed to be the reincarnation of a Buddha. The child must have been sick, for he kept wiping his nose and sniffling as the ceremony dragged on for more than an hour. Two adult monks stood on either side of the child and held him so that he could not run off. Yet, the child kept fidgeting and, understandably, throwing off the heavy crown that the monks kept putting on his head. After a while, I could not watch and left the ceremonial hall, followed by the person who had originally invited me. Then I asked her, "Don't you feel sorry for that child, separated from his mother, being forced to sit in a cold room with strangers touching and holding him?" She nodded. I also asked her, "I have heard that Nepal has many enlightened and revered monks. Yet, it has a fifty percent infant mortality rate and I see beggars on the streets with their limbs cut off on purpose to extract pity and a few coins from passers-by. Do you think that an enlightenment that ignores such plights can be called true enlightenment?" Finally, I told her, "Enlightenment that is reputed to be the salvation, happiness, peace, and freedom for mankind and yet cannot make a positive contribution to the real world has lost its meaning. And enlightenment that has become the object of worship in and of itself has lost even more meaning. Enlightenment that leaves fattened cows to run around on the streets because of religious beliefs while letting infants starve to death is not real enlightenment. Enlightenment that has lost its real-world priority is not enlightenment. Only enlightenment with True Love can be considered enlightenment. Only enlightenment with True Love expressed through reality-based works that contribute positively to society can be considered true enlightenment. These Nepal monks could be enlightened. But as I see it, it is enlightenment without courage or True Love. And ultimately, such enlightenment is not enlightenment at all."

I am not here to criticize any specific culture or religion. I am here to criticize all cultures and religions that fail to break out of the original, suffocating mold and demand that all its followers suffer so that they may pay homage to some

17

old, abstract ideals, no matter how noble they may have been at one time. All cultural paradigms are products of their particular time and history. What arose out of one particular time or situation should not continue to govern what may be a totally different time and situation, especially when such blind faiths lead to real suffering and dilapidation.

What sets the likes of Jesus and the Buddha apart is that they utilized their enlightenment for the betterment of their real-world community. Higher enlightenment is not just finding your True Self, feeling it as part of the Cosmic Soul, and knowing that everything is One. Higher enlightenment is coming back down among the masses and sharing and preaching that knowledge to all the world. Unselfish and giving enlightenment is what True Love is all about. The highest form of enlightenment is in sharing. In teaching. In giving yourself to others selflessly so that others might experience what you have. It is in making a positive change to your immediate world.

Do you think that the Buddha wanted to live in his physical form till he was past eighty years old and go through the hardships, the pain, the hunger, and all the unpleasant necessities that aging brings? Don't you think that he was tempted to just elevate himself into a higher plane of existence once he became enlightened? Of course he was. Can you just imagine the drudgery of life to a being who knows that everything around him is an illusion? But why do you think he came back? For power? For respect? For everlasting fame? What good are these when you know that they are only illusions? Would you be tempted to eat a piece of cake when you knew it was just a clumsy hologram? When you knew that the real thing was just around the corner? Then why did he come back? Simple. True Love for all mankind. He wrenched himself away from his higher existence and came back down among the grime and the filth to get his own hands dirty in order to bring the rest of us up with him. Or at least tell us how. This is the sacrifice he made. This is the True Love he showed. And this is the same love that Jesus showed when he, too, came back down among the masses to show us the way. Jesus' supreme sacrifice didn't lie with the crucifixion. It lay with the fact that he chose to come back and share his enlightenment with the masses, knowing that he would be killed. He came to teach us True Love.

Without knowing our True Selves, we cannot know True Love. So far, we have known only selfish love, egotistical love, controlling love, and domineering love. We have sought to use love as a tool to conquer and win. Even a porcupine loves its young. Even a lowly rodent knows to die for its offspring. Love based on blood is not True Love. Love based on nationality is not love. Love based on color is not True Love. True Love is spiritual love. It is love expressed toward all existence and given form through reality.

Why do we have to seek enlightenment? To recover the True Love in our hearts. By losing the memory of True Love in our hearts, we have fallen from being gods to being animals. Now we need to rejoin the ranks of the divine.

It's time for us, all of humanity, to set a standard for True Love. That True Love is love that loves not only Heaven, Earth, and human, but all of existence. This should be the standard against which all others are measured.

Close your eyes and look deep inside yourself. Ask yourself if you really strived for True Love. Do you know the meaning of True Love? What are the things that are blocking your True Love from surfacing? Could it be that they are doubt, egotism, and lack of respect?

To erect a society based on the standards of True Love. This is *"E-wha Saegae*—Everything-Harmonious World." This is what we have to wish and strive for with all our hearts. This is why I am calling for a Spiritual-Cultural Movement that will sweep the world and act as a seed out of which mass enlightenment can germinate. This is why we need an Enlightenment Revolution.

Why did science and technology advance so quickly in the last century? Because we have become even more anxious and nervous than ever. Competition derives its power from the anxiety of Man. You compete because you are fearful. Through competition, you seek to guarantee your future security. Through competition, everything has become quicker. Everything is aging faster: humans, Heaven, Earth, nature. Even nature needs to take a rest. That means that Earth needs to take a rest soon. Human souls who have completed their journeys will also rest. Everything goes in cycles, without end. After a period of rest, we will start back up again with our collective journey. This is not a prophecy, but common sense. This is not something to fear.

But we should not lie idle and wait. We are here on Earth for a purpose, to recover our sense of True Love. If we do, we will no longer be fearful. Of Final Judgment or anything else. Let's not procrastinate, but get on with our main job.

Enlightenment is True Love.

Yuln'yo

When I was five, I underwent an experience through which I felt the Universal Awareness and the True Love contained therein. I further realized that there existed an invisible stream of energy that flows within our bodies and that this energy binds us to the universe. In fact, the energy that animates our bodies and the energy that animates the universe was from the same stream. And through endless questions and searches, one day I finally heard the voice that spoke the Truth. And realized that this voice was inside me all along.

This voice told me that my body is not me, but mine. It told me that my mind is not me, but mine. It assured me that the Cosmic Mind is my mind and that the Cosmic Energy is my energy. Through this voice I came to feel the all-encompassing rhythm of life. I experienced the light, the sound, and the vibration that formed the source of all life, absorbing and understanding in wonder the Cosmic Order within that governed all things. It is because I wanted to relate to others the vision that I have experienced that I developed and introduced to the world an awareness-raising program called *Dahn Hak*. Brain Respiration can be called the essence of the *Dahn Hak* program.

The eternal Cosmic Order that governs all, this I call *Yuln'yo*. You cannot touch *Yuln'yo,* or smell it or see it. *Yuln'yo* is the essence of the order that has governed all life since the beginning, having itself no beginning or end. *Yuln'yo* is not some cold set of physical laws that dictates the interactions of matter, but a pulsating, warm consciousness that envelops and gathers all. *Yuln'yo* expresses itself through light, sound, and vibration that form the natural symphony of the cosmos. We can most immediately feel the power of *Yuln'yo* through our heartbeats, the steady and faithful pounding that started in the womb and is now echoing through the universe. This is the rhythm of life. Through this rhythm, we can join the everlasting harmony of the cosmos. And as we truly realize the beauty of our own lives, we will discover *Yuln'yo*. *Yuln'yo* loves, in the purest and truest sense of the word. This is the enormity and the purity of what I have experienced. This is what I want you to experience. And this is what I want the whole of humanity to experience.

When you recover *Yuln'yo*, you recover your balance. Up to now, the standards by which you have lived were not your own but those of others. You lived your life not to recover your lost inner balance, but to pursue wealth, fame, and power, leading to a twisted sense of sight and judgment. However, by grabbing hold of the lifeline of *Yuln'yo,* you can regain your inner balance and feel absolute happiness and peace. It's easy to tell if you have *Yuln'yo* in your heart, for your mouth will pour forth a stream of blessings and praises that make yourself and all others feel hope and love. If *Yuln'yo* is lost in your heart, your words will hurt others with negativity and spite. When you hold *Yuln'yo* in your heart, you are breathing with the cosmos and living in harmony with Heaven, Earth, and humanity. *Yuln'yo* is not something you buy with money or await with patience. *Yuln'yo* is something you just accept from within yourself. *Yuln'yo* is the Cosmic Order. *Yuln'yo* is True Love. *Yuln'yo* is the Creator Within.

In studying and absorbing the various spiritual traditions of the world, a commonality emerges, bubbling to the top through the sheer power of its universality and truth, almost a gentle clamor that refuses to be ignored whether embedded in the unpretentious teachings of Jesus, ingrained in the patient wisdom of the Buddha, or resonated in the fiery speech of Muhammad. The wording or the emphasis may differ, but this commonality also emerges in the rustic wisdom of fables, the slow rolling of native chants, and even in the quaint, traditional games that children learn to play during the major holidays of the world. What is this common theme? That there exists a Universal Awareness, a Cosmic Mind that watches over all of us with patience and love that we cannot intellectually comprehend, yet we instinctively feel. That through this Cosmic Mind, we are subject to the same and eternal Cosmic Order that governs the universe. This is what I call *Yuln'yo*. Therein lies the source for everything that there is, ever was, and ever will be. Through this Cosmic Mind, we are all interconnected and inseparable from one another. We are all One, in the grandest fashion imaginable.

This is not just an abstract saying. This is the most concrete and realistic saying that there is. This Truth has the power to affect everything in our lives. This Truth is the force that animates this universe. It is this Truth that can satisfy our deepest longings, our deepest suspicions, and our deepest curiosity about our origins, our goals, and our significance. It is this Truth that will open up the gateway to higher dimensions, to higher levels of awareness.

We have always known on some level that there exists something more than physical life, something that lies beyond the realm of space and time. In our most creative or loving or selfless moments, we have glimpsed and felt this force. Each of us is constantly being drawn back to this force because we instinctively feel it is this that animates us, nurtures us, and gives us our ultimate meaning and order in life. As we are all part of this force, thus we are all One. It is simple, profound; and the message already has been told to us countless times by thousands of sages and prophets spanning all of human history, including the very ones who are active today. It is a Truth that, if embedded into the collective human consciousness and acted upon, will solve the world's most pressing problems in an instant. For, how could you let a Sudanese baby starve to death while throwing away your spoiled food, watch a Vietnamese woman be brutalized while making love to your wife, and send Iraqi boys to be mowed down by bullets while throwing birthday parties for your own kids, if you truly realize that we are all One? And if this Truth is applied beyond the realm of immediate human experiences, we will realize that we are not only synonymous with the planet we live on, but synonymous with this universe that we inhabit.

Put this way, it sounds so obvious and simple. The problem so far has not been that we don't have access to the highest of Truths; the problem is that we just don't get it. The problem is not the message. The problem is in the method of the delivery. How do we make people realize and act upon this Truth?

Religions have been trying for thousands of years and have failed. In fact, through organizational religions, this simple Truth has in many cases been distorted, and access to it denied to the masses. Truth be told, organized religions are the most undemocratic and elitist organizations around. They imply that you cannot go to Heaven, enter nirvana, or attain enlightenment unless you go through one of them, the clergy. Why does there have to be a clear delineation between the congregation and the clergy? Between the shepherd and the sheep? Because the clergy's status depends on you remaining a meek sheep, dependent upon them to dole out spiritual favors. You could be a better person than any of them, yet you have to bow down because of rules generated to keep the clergy in a position of status. But status is a man-made affectation, which the truly enlightened do not need. So what does that tell us about organized religions? That they are just like any other form of man-made organization, primarily trying to perpetuate their own power and foster a sense of the "Other." Unless current religions expand to become truly inclusive and accepting, they cannot lead us to the Truth. For some, very select people, maybe. But not for the majority of us.

What about the enlightened ones? From the desert and mountaintops, prophets have been shouting out the dire consequences of not heeding the Truth for millennia, but have people listened? What happened to the prophets' messages after they passed away? They have been obscured, twisted, and doled out in fragments by the religions that have sprung up from the traces of their personalities, all competing with each other on the alleged superiority of their own ways to the same Truth. And how many people have been killed in the process of this competition and the religious wars that have sprung from it? How many continue to be killed?

The solution is not more enlightened ones. We have arrived at a spiritual fork in the road taken by humanity. We no longer need one or two or even one thousand enlightened beings telling us what the Truth is. The time for isolated, individual enlightenment is over. The time for wise beings shouting at us from the mountaintops is over. What we need now to change humanity's fortunes is a mass enlightenment, a mass spiritual awakening in which millions upon millions of people around the globe truly realize that we are One. We need to raise the collective consciousness of the whole human race, not just one or two people. And we surely need this change, for we are currently headed toward a certain disaster. You don't have to be enlightened to see that.

How do we do that? How do we make people realize that Cosmic Mind is our minds and that Cosmic Energy is our energy and that we are all part of this majestic Cosmic Order? How do we make people realize that we are One in *Yuln'yo,* much the same way we realize that we need to breathe to live? How do we make this knowledge instinctive? Or more accurately, how do we cause this already instinctive knowledge to surface to our immediate awareness and be acted upon consciously? We can't teach through words, for this is not something that can be understood intellectually. History has proven that the various political and economic systems have proven ineffective in teaching people this Truth, if even attempted. Even religions have failed, maybe not with certain select individuals, but certainly on a massive scale. So, how do we awaken the spirituality that we know lies within us? How do we get in touch with the divinity, the same, all-encompassing divinity, that we all share? How?

Energy is the answer. Or *Ki,* in Eastern traditions. This is the key element that has been lacking in the spiritual traditions of the world. Energy is what connects the body, mind, and spirit. It is the common bond that holds the three together, while not being limited to any single form. And energy can be the path through which ordinary people can feel the connection to *Chunji Kiun,* or the Cosmic Energy. The source whence we all came. *Yuln'yo.*

Certainly, there have been many practices throughout history that recognized and sought to develop the energy system of the body. In fact, this is the ultimate goal of many martial arts in Asia: to strengthen the body by utilizing the energy flow that animates the physical body. But we have never before used this energy flow in a systematic way to strengthen our spiritual body. We have never purposefully utilized the energy flow that circulates through our bodies to connect our life force to the Cosmic Force and thereby to everything and everyone—realizing the Oneness not on an intellectual or even philosophical plane, but feeling it with every single fiber of our being, imprinted onto every one of our cells through a profound experience.

Imagine lecturing about water to someone who has never seen, felt, or touched it. Imagine describing the feel, taste, texture, density, and everything else that makes up water in order to make this person understand what water is. Now imagine lifting up this person and throwing him into a pool. Which do you think will be more effective in teaching him what water truly is? Personal experience, personal connection to the Oneness, is the key to enlightenment.

Energy is the natural bridge that connects the body, mind, and spirit. It is the perfect bridge to allow people to truly experience the universality of their existence. You no longer have to enter a monastery in high, secluded mountains to reach enlightenment. You don't have to pray in the desert for forty days and forty nights to reach God. The time for elitist enlightenment is over. The time for the chosen few is over. The whole of humanity needs to realize the Truth for us to change the fortune of the human race. This is not an option. This is not even a matter of life or death. It's far more important. This is a matter of the survival of our higher existence. And *Ki* can show us the way.

But what vehicle would we use to cross this bridge? There lies the most important message of this book. At this point, I would like to introduce you to Brain Respiration.

Brain Respiration is a revolutionary relaxation and guided meditation technique that will allow you to feel the *Ki* energy flowing throughout your body, and eventually tap into the most powerful reservoir of energy in your physical body: your brain. You will use your brain to raise your awareness to the point at which you can consciously communicate with the Cosmic Mind. You will use your brain for the fulfillment of your spiritual needs. You will learn use your brain to truly experience the Oneness, not just in words, but in actuality. Believe me, that experience will change your outlook on life.

Enlightenment Revolution

The primary aim of an Enlightenment Revolution is to make people realize their potential for enlightenment. That enlightenment is not for the select few. That enlightenment can occur in everyday life. That mass enlightenment is the only way to solve today's widespread ills. But mass enlightenment starts with the individuals. When enough individuals are enlightened, only then do you have a mass enlightenment. But in our current world, it is impossible for large numbers of people to forsake everything and devote their everyday lives only to the purpose of enlightenment. People need something that they can use in their everyday lives to lead them to a profound, mind-awakening spiritual experience of *Yuln'yo*.

The secondary aim of an Enlightenment Revolution is to introduce and share the basic concepts and techniques through which we can use *Ki* energy to experience this Oneness. To experience *Yuln'yo*. To see the light, hear the sound, and feel the vibration that forms the source of all life and energy. These concepts and techniques are what constitute Brain Respiration.

My sincere hope is that you read this book not only as an exhortation to push you to greater spiritual heights, but as a matter-of-fact guide to opening yourself up to the divine potential that lies within by using Brain Respiration. Through Brain Respiration, you will become a New Human, a spiritual person whose primary goal is to create harmony. And when enough New Humans join together in a worldwide Spiritual-Cultural Movement, we will effect the grandest revolution in the history of humankind, a revolution that will usher in a new era of spiritualism.

A Personal Story— Walking in Snow

My first experience with *Ki* came when I was five years old in rural South Korea. South Korea in the fifties was not a pleasant place to live, due to the devastation left by the Korean War between 1950 and 1953. Yet, when I close my eyes and think back, the image of my mother, my father, the babbling of the stream, the deafening sounds of the cicadas, and the noise of my friends playing together form a beautiful composite picture that lingers wistfully.

One day, my mother woke me early in the morning, in panic because she had forgotten that her mother-in-law's birthday was that day. Forgetting your mother-in-law's birthday was something that just didn't happen in those days. And my paternal grandmother had a reputation for being a tiger.

It's a Korean tradition to cook a seaweed and meat broth on someone's birthday. But we had no meat in our house. Not only was meat rare in those days, but the nearest butcher was over five miles away through rough, mountainous terrain, not to mention the knee-deep snow that covered the trails. But when I saw how my mother was panicking, I suddenly volunteered to go to the butcher to buy a pound of meat. And in her panic and in the absence of my father, she actually gave permission to her five-year-old son to go alone in the middle of winter.

The way to the mini-market where the butcher had a shop passed by a public cemetery and underground caves that were treacherously hidden in the snow. One misstep, and you would never be found till spring. It wasn't a pleasant stroll, by any means. But I had no time for these thoughts, for I had only my mother's panicked face in my head, and how I had to go buy the meat so that my mother wouldn't be horribly embarrassed. It was only years later when I realized that such feeling of unselfish love most often triggers a palpable experience of *Ki* energy.

And this is where it gets interesting and why it has remained with me for all those years. As I walked along the path with the snow knee-high, I didn't leave any foot marks. I just sort of sailed along. Without footprints, although the snow was fresh and fluffy. And I felt this incredible warmth all around me, as if the air itself was a warm blanket. I hummed as I raced along the snow-covered path and knocked on the door of the butcher shop, which hadn't even opened yet. But the drowsiness and grouchiness of the butcher disappeared when he saw me, and he gave me double the weight for the same price, saying that I was a nice boy for doing errands so early in the morning. Perhaps he was affected by the warmth of positive energy filling my heart.

Then, as I raced back toward my house, I moved into a trancelike state in which I found myself looking down at myself skipping along the snow. I asked, "What am I doing here?" Not, "What am I doing by doing errands in the early morning when it's freezing out?" but, "What am I doing here with such and such mother and father and living in such a place with such and such family members and friends?" I felt as if the true me had awakened a little disoriented and was asking where it was. It was at this point that I discovered an ability that allowed me to see myself beyond the confines of current societal norms and relationships into who I truly was, and to ask the really important questions that we all eventually ask: "Why am I here at this particular time and place?" and "What is my life all about?"

And when I got back to my house, my mother greeted me with a look of delight and shock. The delight because I had brought back the meat. The shock because it had taken me less than half the time it would take a grown-up man to travel the same distance. This was my first experience with *Ki* energy, and its power to not only create certain physical manifestations but to get me in touch with my True Self.

Individual Enlightenment— Brain Respiration

Why Do We
Need Enlightenment?

Imagine a bowl of white rice and two hungry men. One man prefers eating the rice by digging in and spooning it to his mouth as quickly as possible, in a very haphazard way. Another man prefers using the spoon to gently scrape layer by layer off from the top until he reaches the bottom of the bowl, in a very meticulous fashion. Whose is the better way? I guess that depends on your personality. If you have a quick temper, you might prefer the former. If you are a controlling type, you might prefer the latter. It's all the same. The rice reaches your mouth the same both ways. There is absolutely no difference except in style.

Now imagine that the two men above get into an argument over the different merits of their own peculiar eating habits. The first man thinks that it doesn't matter how you eat the damn rice, since it's all going to be eaten in a few minutes anyway. The second man stresses the need for a certain decorum even when doing things as commonplace as eating rice. The argument gets heated. The first man accuses the second of being controlling and arrogant while the second man counteraccuses the first one of being sloppy and ignorant. The argument turns into fistfight, and during this fight the bowl of rice drops from the table and breaks into a thousand pieces, scattering the tiny, white pebbles of rice all over the floor.

Now neither of them can eat, and they remain hungry. Why? Because they both lost sight of what's really important—the bowl of rice itself. In trying to declare the superiority of their respective positions, they both wind up in inferior positions. In trying to win individually, they have lost collectively.

That is a very simple fable, but one that describes our present society quite accurately. For example, say that the first man represents capitalism and the second man socialism. What is the difference between these two great ideologies? Different ways to eat the same bowl of rice. It's only a matter of a difference of opinion for the same thing. Neither one is good or evil. Neither one is correct or wrong. And neither one is what's most important. The bowl of rice is. Yet, we inevitably get into an argument which will eventually lead into a fight, breaking that bowl of rice. It would be comic if it weren't so costly and tragic.

Currently, capitalism is the acknowledged winner. Harking back to our fable, let's now put a different ending to the story. Say the bowl didn't drop and that the person who eats rice one particular way ate most of the rice. Good, you say? At least one person got to fill his belly? But what about the other person? Couldn't these two have shared the bowl equally and assuaged their hunger together? Did one have to starve for the other to be satisfied? Let's say that the winner represents capitalism and the loser socialism. How would you feel when you realized that the other person has to do without so that you could do with just a little bit more? Would you feel justified because you were better, faster, and smarter? Is it a case of the survival of the fittest?

We can do far better than this. It is in our nature to do far better than this.

What about the differences between Catholics and Protestants? Christians and Jews? Blacks and whites? It is just a matter of different ways of eating the same bowl of rice.

Am I oversimplifying things? I wish I were. But in the greater scheme of things, our most dramatic and historical differences turn out to be the most trivial. But it is a triviality with brutal and tragic results. If we added up the numbers of human beings killed because of these differences, the zeros would fill this page. How about the cruelty? The Crusaders slitting the bellies of women and children alike in their religious fervor. The Catholic and Protestant mobs rounding up and forcing the Jews to kiss the hind end of the hogs in the middle of the town square before burning them to death. The Romans forcing the Christians into an arena to be brutalized and eaten alive by a pack of hungry lions in front of thousands of crazed spectators. The invading Japanese army cutting off the ears and noses of the residents of a Korean town for daring to put up a fight—a mound of earth where the cut-off ears and noses are buried sits in the middle of Tokyo today as a testament to human cruelty.

When we were spearing innocent and helpless babies in the name of God, do you think that He was truly happy? When hot blood was spilt, innards pulled out, babies' heads dashed, and other unspeakable cruelties perpetrated in the name of God, do you think He was cheering on the sidelines for His team? How could religion, with such noble goals, deteriorate into something so evil? Because these things happened in the Middle Ages, when our ancestors were ignorant savages?

Don't think so. Are we doing any better now? With the advent of the Industrial Revolution and now the Information Revolution, our physical lives have certainly become more comfortable. We can fly to the other side of the Earth in a few hours, talk to someone over the Internet in real time, and have delicious meals after five minutes in a microwave oven. We can also destroy the world many upon many times over, kill more people than ever with a single blast, and irrevocably damage the ozone layer, rain forests, and oceans with our insatiable appetite for more. And in the midst of this plenty, we still can't eradicate hunger, do without wars, prevent injustices, or solve any of the higher problems that have been plaguing humankind since the beginning of history. An old lady is killed for her Social Security check—beaten, raped, and smothered to death. A fourteen-year-old kid slits the throat of another fourteen-year-old for a vial of crack. A mother drowns her two little boys by locking them inside a car and driving the car into a lake. And you want to scream, "Why?"

Because we are still trying to figure out how to divide up the same bowl of rice. We still haven't widened our sight enough to see the bowl itself. We are still stuck in this paradigm of competition that we've been living in since recorded history. We are searching for our self-worth through competition. When we win, we feel good about ourselves. When we lose, we feel bad. So, we want to win. At all costs. And the other people be damned. Because we want to win in this competition called life, we argue about the bowl of rice and go hungry as a result. That is how the world around us divides us up: in order to be anybody in this world, to feel good about yourself, to merely survive, you have to compete, and how can you tell who the winner is? The winner is the one with the most toys. The best houses, more cars, more women, more fame, more recognition, and more of everything. Materialism is a system of living that uses competition to create a caste system of winners and losers.

The insidious catch is that the competition is self-sustaining and spirals upward until everyone is eventually a loser. There will always be someone who runs when you walk, and who flies when you run. Materialism is a system of living that creates losers out of all of us.

If a social system requires that we be winners to feel self-worth, what happens to the feelings of self-worth of the losers, who are left out of the social system as outcasts and pariahs. No wonder so many people feel anxious and nervous, because they know deep down inside that they will be left out of the loop eventually, if they are not already.

Those who are branded losers in this competition are doomed to feel fear and despair. In midst of this despair, they lose touch with their True Self, their inherent goodness, and fall into the trap of hate and revenge at what they perceive as those things and people that have made them feel this way. Then they strike out, causing more hate and destruction. This is why seemingly normal kids take out guns and shoot their classmates. This is why there will be an ever-increasing number of rapes, murders, and other hate crimes in the world. Here and there you might see a temporary drop in crime statistics, but it will only be temporary because it is our whole system that is making people into criminals. Acting out their hatred at the same time they search for a modicum of self-worth even in despair, people will try mind-altering drugs, hurt others, and seek to destroy.

Why do people lash out in such ways when they feel like losers? Because their basic needs are not being met. We all have three instinctive needs that ache to be fulfilled: need for safety, need for recognition, and need for control. All human relationships in our current society are impacted by these three driving needs.

The need for safety or stability is the most basic of them all. People feel rage and anger when something or someone threatens their safety, whether it be physical safety, economic stability, or social stature. If they are helpless against the threats, they fall into fear and despair.

People also have a need to be acknowledged or recognized for their worth. If you are recognized, you feel good. If you are not, you don't. You'd do almost anything to be recognized. In one way or another, your current situation is the sum of all the things that you have done to satisfy your needs for safety and recognition. You have smiled in order to maintain your sense of safety and stability, you have striven to be diligent to be recognized, and you have tried to be responsible in order to maintain a certain status in life.

Finally, people have a need to dominate or control. When someone agrees and follows your lead, he or she is likable. When someone disagrees with you, he or she is not so likable.

There are many people who offer an illegal or unethical favor in return for bribes. In general, these people who take bribes are considered immoral, somehow below the norm of human behavior. But are they really that different from the rest of us upstanding citizens? If someone flatters you and reinforces your basic need to feel safe and recognized, wouldn't you be more apt to look upon him kindly, no matter what he may be asking? If someone attacks these basic needs, would you feel kindly toward that person no matter how noble he might be? There are really no huge differences between people. We feel happy or sad each day depending how our three basic needs are satisfied.

Try analyzing yourself by applying these three needs to your situation. What are you really happy or sad about? I want you to look deep inside yourself. You will find that everything you have felt and done will be because of these three needs. That's why losing in a competition hurts so much. Because losing directly attacks these three needs that are aching to be fulfilled.

But there is one need that goes beyond the three that we have just discussed. This need comes not from our physical selves, but from our spiritual underpinnings. Therefore, it goes deeper than an instinct. It is part of our spiritual being. This is our need for a connection to others based on harmony and love. In the midst of a hectic day, have you ever stopped for a second or two and asked yourself how nice it would be to be forever free of worries and always feel loved? If so, it wasn't any weakness on your part. It was your spiritual self reminding you that you have something better to strive for than constant competition. And how do we satisfy this need? By realizing that we are truly everlasting, and that we are part of something so omnipotent, omniscient, and forever that we couldn't possibly be lacking anything or asking for more. By realizing that we are constantly enveloped inside this spiritual cocoon that makes up the universe. By knowing that we are part of the Oneness of *Yuln'yo.* If you truly experience this connection just once, it will obliterate any other small needs that you might seek to fulfill. Why do you need one more car or need your boss's approval when you know that you are an inherent part of something so grand? Would you really quibble over pennies when you have just found out that you've won ten million dollars?

But you have to learn to let go of your three basic needs first. You have to make that choice to let them go. It is a thief's mentality to want to hold on to one while striving to have another. You have to make a clean choice. If you can't make up your mind where your ultimate destination will be, how can you get there? You won't feel any real changes until you have made a clear choice in mind and deed.

We give in to our needs for safety, recognition, and control when we have lost touch with the greater safety that the realization of Oneness can provide. We give in to our petty needs when we lose sense of our spiritual umbilical cord and immerse ourselves in this competition-driven society, deluding ourselves that competition is the fairest form of collective interaction, that the strongest and best should prosper—that it *should* be the "survival of the fittest." And through this constant, ruthless competition, we have lost an overall sense of cooperation, trust, and harmony while constantly being fearful and anxious, no matter how much wealth or status we have accumulated. We will never truly be rid of our fear and anxiety unless we consciously reestablish this connection between the cosmos and ourselves.

Only when this system of self-worth through competition changes into self-worth through harmony will we create a truly happy and fair society. This requires a revolution in spirituality—a mass enlightenment that can shift the sense of what living is all about. We have to shift the competitive social paradigm that has governed us since the beginning of recorded history. When our collective awareness has evolved high enough to effect this shift, then we will feel the great universal love that has always enveloped us. This is the reason for an Enlightenment Revolution.

The ills of this society cannot be cured by just tweaking the system here and there. It is futile to pass more laws, no matter how fair-minded and well-intentioned, to solve today's problems, because they seek to work without changing the whole paradigm. Politics, economies, cultures, and religions all have professed to seek love, harmony, and cooperation, but have failed because they could not go beyond the competition paradigm with which we all have been burdened. Therefore, each one of these professes to be the only "correct way" or the only "direct line to God" and deride and despise the "others" for not agreeing.

This will not do anymore. In order to bring about an upshift in collective human consciousness, we need an impetus, a Spiritual-Cultural Movement that will awaken people to their divinity within. This movement will start with each one of us feeling our connection to the cosmos in such an undeniable way that we could never again forget that we are truly One. If enough people realize this and act out what naturally follows, then the human species is destined to create a social paradigm based on love, harmony, and cooperation.

The process is individual enlightenment, group enlightenment, human enlightenment.

Let us now all embark upon this road that will start out with individual enlightenment, and then join together to form a New Human Society before pushing forth with the power of True Self and True Love to effect a total spiritual transformation of humanity. Only when we have collectively raised our spiritual awareness to realize that we are part of the Cosmic Awareness will we reach our noblest of goals.

We can begin our journey on this road by becoming aware of the *Ki* life energy that surrounds and animates us, the bridge to the oneness of the cosmos. And we will cross this bridge by using our brains. By letting our brains breathe.

Through Brain Respiration.

Information Makes
Us Who We Are

How would you answer when someone asks you, "What's your favorite flower?" How about, "What's your favorite color?"

If you answer, "I like roses," or "I like blue," who is this "I" you are talking about? What is this "I" entity that decided that it liked roses and the color blue? This entity is the compilation of information that is in your head. A human being is an amalgamation of countless pieces of information. The human awareness of "me" consists of what my name is, how old I am, what my favorite color is, what my favorite flower is, what the happiest moment in my life was, what my future dream is, and so on. This compilation of sorted information is what differentiates us from one another.

Information, depending upon the route through which we absorb it, can be divided into three categories: genetic information, intellectual information, and experiential information. Genetic information is carried by the sperm of the father and the ovum of the mother. It is passed down to us by our collective ancestors through countless years of refinement. Intellectual information is information that we get through outside sources such as books, education, movies, television, and all manner of external media. It is an indirect form of information. Experiential information is information that we

personally feel and absorb through direct experience or con-
frontation with an event. It is a direct form of information.

Information is not all believable or trustworthy. Some has
been verified and some hasn't. There is information that is in
the midst of the verification process, information that is correct, and information that has been proven incorrect. There is
information that we can all agree on. Then there is information that only applies to a few groups. For example, a few
years back I took a trip to Katmandu in Nepal and saw fattened cows walking the streets freely and people stepping out
of their way. This, in a country with an infant mortality rate
higher than fifty percent. There were babies starving to death
and crippled beggars on the streets with their limbs purposely
mutilated to attract pity, yet the cows couldn't be touched
because they were considered sacred by the particular sect of
Buddhism that populated the land. As I observed this scene,
I realized anew how much control a set of information called
"religion" exercises over human behavior.

In the Christian Bible, the serpent is an embodiment of
evil for having seduced Eve into eating the fruit from the Tree
of Knowledge. Therefore, in the West, the snake is considered
evil and is subjected to stoning, spearing, and all other sorts
of lethal abuse. In the East, on the other hand, the snake is
reputed to be good for sexual stamina. A captured snake is
eviscerated and its innards taken out and preserved to be sold
on the market at outrageous prices. A snake is a precious
commodity in the East while it is Satan in the West—the
contrasting results of different information.

Living as we are in a sea of information, we need to be able
to differentiate the various types of information as well. The most
trustworthy information is the type we get through direct experience. This is done by using your brain. And Brain Respiration is
a tool with which you can do it more effectively, a superior information processing protocol. Brain Respiration is an experiential
information processing protocol through which you can control
the flow of your information, rather than be controlled by it.

The type of information you hold can determine how you speak, how you think, and what jobs you hold. A doctor has the information he needs to cure diseases, and a lawyer has the information to deal with legal matters. It could even be said that a person's worth can be decided by the quality and quantity of information that he or she holds. Therefore, we put a value on a person through a diploma or a certificate. What type of information do you have? How much of that information do you have? How valuable or esoteric is that information? The answers to these questions place a value on your life. A person with much information that is useless will not be considered very worthy in general society.

It is time we examine whether the standard by which we judge the value of a person's information is itself correct. So far we have decided on the value of a person through his or her education level, occupation, family background, wealth, and other external factors instead of asking about the person's value system or life philosophy. However, the true value of a person depends on the positive contribution that he or she makes to society. A person who may be talented and smart but is harmful to the general well-being of the society is a value-less person. People in the highest positions of power, such as the President, Speaker of the House, or CEO of the largest corporation in the world, are valueless if they don't contribute positively to society. They actually have a heavier obligation to make a positive change, for they are in positions to do so. Only if they do will they be living up to their true worth. A person who has a lot of positive information inside to contribute to society can be said to have a higher spiritual awareness. However, we don't usually think that we have the right or the ability to change the set of information we have gathered that makes up who we are as human beings. We have unconsciously absorbed the pieces of information that have flowed into us and passively incorporated them into who we are without question or complaint. We are fooled into thinking that this bunch of information is actually us. Take a flea and put it into a bottle with a glass top. After a few times of jumping up and bumping into the glass top, the flea will eventually jump only so high that it doesn't hit the top anymore, even if you take the top off later. We human beings don't have this glass top. The only limitation we have is the false information that we hold on to as if it were the truth. We *imagine* this glass top to be real for ourselves. We don't recognize that we have the choice to make it disappear and to free ourselves. It's a choice.

The choice to be free can only be actualized though a purposeful decision to break out of the stifling grasp of false information and to courageously stay the course. And your brain will give you the power to do this.

Everyone has a brain, but only a few know how to use their brains well. The brain is the father of all computers. From the brain came the computer, language, religion, culture, history, laws, and everything that makes up the Age of Materialism in which we live today. The history of mankind developed through our brains. Everything that surrounds us today is a by-product of how we have used our brains. When you know human brains, you know human beings. Today, the most advanced nations in the world are competing against one another to fund research that delves deeper into the mystery that is our brain. However, those research studies generally concentrate on the biological and structural nature of the brain. Little research deals with how to develop methods to use our brains better.

Yet, the most important issue is not how brains function, but how to use our brains to their fullest potential. A typical human being is said to use only five to ten percent of his or her brain potential. Even Einstein is reputed to have used only ten percent of his brain potential. This is akin to using the CRAY Supercomputer to run a word processing program. How to develop the hidden potential of our brain to use to better the quality of our collective lives? That is the research subject for the twenty-first century!

There are many known functions of the brain that we are not utilizing well even now, although we know about them. Chief among these is the information-processing power of the brain. Just as we can input and delete information in regular computers, we can input and delete information in our brains. And our brains have the amazing capability to create information—something that not even the most advanced computer can emulate.

Just imagine how nice it would be to rid of bad, negative, and useless information that is cluttering up your brain. Of course, human brains do naturally forget information through diseases and old age, but information that is accompanied by emotional turmoil or shock does not go away as easily. A person who had been embarrassed singing a song as a child will still recall it with fresh vividness when he is an adult, making him reluctant to sing, even though he might be a good singer. Negative information is just like a computer virus, destroying and wreaking havoc once inside.

Up to now, we have generally been ruled by our information. A fortuitous meeting with a good piece of information may change our lives for the better, while a bad piece of information can lead us down a path of self-destruction. On the strength of one piece of information, we may laugh with joy or cry with grief. It is time to control the flow of information, not be controlled by it. This is only possible when we believe in the power of our own brain and utilize it. Everyone has a brain, but few know how to fully use it. The brain is a funny machine in that it runs smoother and does more things the more you use it.

When you input positive information into the brain, it will sparkle with creativity and hum with efficiency. For instance, if you tell someone, "You have come into this world to save the Earth and open up a new era of spirituality and peace in the twenty-first century. Do you accept this?" If the person says, "Yes," his brain will perk up and purr with delight. "No," and his brain will contract upon itself and darken as it shuts down its higher powers. But saving the Earth does not have to be a grand undertaking. Picking up one more loose piece of trash or saying one more nice thing to your neighbor also qualifies.

The quality of our lives depends on what type of information we feed and program into our brains. When you erase the self-defeating information that says you are here on earth to pass the time as best as you can, and replace it with the information that urges you to solve humankind's problems and save the world, your spiritual awareness will jump into a higher plane at that instant. Our most intractable problems can suddenly dissolve, depending upon the type of information that we input into our brains. *Brain Respiration is a method that seeks to elevate a person's spiritual awareness by teaching him or her how to control the type of information that remains in the brain.*

The distinctiveness of Brain Respiration lies in the fact that it is the first training program in the world *designed to develop the hidden potential of your brain.* The purpose for the development of Brain Respiration is to advance the evolution of human consciousness and usher in a new era of worldwide spirituality in the new millennium.

A human being by himself is not good or evil. His value system, philosophy, religion, and even personality are decided by the type of information he has absorbed growing up. Now, through Brain Respiration, we can trace back the route of this various information and change it if we wish—not though some form of hypnosis or brainwashing done by a third party to satisfy some petty need to control. Brain Respiration is done by your own hands, through your own choice, for the advancement of your own spiritual awareness, and for the betterment of yourself and all humankind. Such is the ultimate goal of Brain Respiration.

Originally, your brain did not have a concept of good or evil. It was pure innocence personified. Whether you wanted it to or not, this society has filled your brain with information that has defined good and evil, delineated between mine and yours, and created other various value judgments that you make every day. The "I" has become a passive compilation of various information that has been fed you. When someone asks, "Who are you?" you tell him your name. When someone else asks "Who are you?" you tell him your occupation. However, your name and your job are not who you truly are.

Religion is another piece of information that has been embedded into your brain. Even life and death are just pieces of information that are occupying your brain. When you erase all the information in your brain, you will be left with just the brain itself, and the source of all life. This doesn't mean that you will become amnesiac. It means that you will be free of all the emotional baggage that comes with the information you have received and will be able to look at it with a truly fresh and objective perspective, ultimately using this information to make positive changes to your life.

Brain Respiration purports to allow someone to be the true master of his or her own brain by controlling the quality of information that is input and deleted. It purports to tell everyone that the brain is just another tool that human beings can use to better their lives. Depending on how you use this tool, the quality of your material life and—far more important—the quality of your spiritual life will change for the better.

Brain Respiration is a training regimen maximized to meet the needs of the twenty-first century. Through Brain Respiration, you will obtain physical health, feel mental peace, and ultimately experience that the Creator lives within you. Brain Respiration is the tool you can use to obtain enlightenment in your everyday life. To find your True Self. To recover True Love.

Brain Respiration is the essence of the Enlightenment Revolution.

Three Layers of the Brain

To utilize your brain in the manner described before, you need to be familiar with the rudimentary facts about our brains. You don't have to be familiar with the various specific names for the different and intricate parts. You just need to know that the brain is divided into three layers. The outermost layer is the neocortex. The middle layer is the cerebral limbic system. And the innermost layer is the brain stem.

On the scale of human history, the neocortex is the youngest of all the three layers, coming into being relatively recently. The neocortex is mainly responsible for logic deduction, reasoning analysis, memory, and creativity. With the development of the neocortex, humans have been able to develop languages, create ideologies and religions, write laws, and raise up civilizations. In a word, the neocortex is what separates human beings from other animals in biological terms. The neocortex has the ability to control our basic instincts, sometimes going too far to the point of suppressing our natural survival instincts. The neocortex is the part of us most responsible for the material world we live in today.

The cerebral limbic system is the domain of emotions and appetites. Within the cerebral limbic system arises our need for food, appetite for sex, and various emotions such as joy, anger, grief, and love. Within the cerebral limbic system also lies the mechanism for controlling the five senses. With the rapid development of the neocortex in humans, the cerebral limbic system has decreased in relative size—it is comparatively less developed than that of animals such as dogs and cats. We have better pneumonic ability, but a dog can smell far better than we can. We can reason, but we cannot see the pupil dilation of a rodent from a hundred meters in the air, as an eagle can.

The cerebral limbic system and the neocortex have an interesting relationship. Imagine a child walking in front of a vegetable store who spies a delicious-looking apple. The cerebral limbic system will demand that the child grab and eat the apple. However, the neocortex, with its reasoning ability, will respond thus after checking how much is in the pocket, "We can't eat it right now because we don't have enough money to buy it." The cerebral limbic system will then whine that it wants the apple right at this moment. But the neocortex will reply, "Wait till we get home and ask Mom for money to buy the apple. Just hold on awhile."

The neocortex thus controls the basic needs and appetites that the cerebral limbic system demands be met by logically weighing the options and conditions available. It is a fine balance that has to be maintained between the needs of the cerebral limbic system and the control of the neocortex. If that control is too tight, the cerebral limbic system can translate the lack of satisfaction into anger, stress, and other emotional outbursts. An individual's personality is partially dependent on the level of balance between these two parts of our brain. Too much neocortex will leave a person introverted and a compulsive perfectionist. Too much cerebral limbic system will leave a person too intent upon instant gratification and generally not suitable for company. Only when these two parts converse well with each other and maintain a nice balance can happiness and health reign.

More important than the neocortex and the cerebral limbic system combined is the brain stem. The brain stem is in charge of the autonomic nervous system responsible for running the basic life functions of the body, including digestion, respiration, and circulation. It is the least known and yet the most important part of our brain. The brain stem never rests. It works from the day we are born until the day we die. The heart beats ceaselessly and the lung expands and contracts without rest, giving us the breath of life. What would happen if the brain stem decided to take a rest? It can't. The neocortex and the cerebral limbic system can rest, but not the brain stem. Just as the Cosmic Order makes the Earth go around the Sun and the seasons turn, the brain stem keeps the machinery of the body going—mutely, efficiently, and without expectation. It doesn't distinguish between evil or good. It does its work equally well whether in the body of a mass murderer or in the body of a saint. Maybe that's why the brain stem is called the "Realm of the Creator."

The work that the brain stem does cannot be controlled or even sensed by the neocortex. All the essential functions of the body are controlled by the brain stem. If we had to consciously sense and control every little thing that the brain stem does, we wouldn't be able to do anything else for fear of killing ourselves through neglect or misstep. We can get a sense of the Creator's benevolent magic in the separation of the brain stem from the neocortex. Imagine if our basic life functions were affected by the type of information that comes into our heads. A harsh word from our boss and we would have trouble breathing. A kiss from a lover will make our hearts overload. As it now stands, thank God we have the cerebral limbic system to act as a barrier between the neocortex and the brain stem. We don't have to think about staying alive. We just do.

But it is in the brain stem that the most inexplicable and seemingly impossible things may happen. For a while the cerebral limbic system acts as a buffer that shields the brain stem from the information processed in the neocortex. But a piece of information that is one hundred percent believable or trustworthy can break through the buffer zone straight into the brain stem. Normally, when information comes in, the neocortex examines it with skepticism and reason. However, something that absolutely is believed to be correct or true can be delivered directly to the brain stem. For example, a woman might faint upon hearing from an authorative source that her mother has died in a horrible traffic accident. The capacity to make a body lose consciousness is in the brain stem. This tragic piece of information went straight to the brain stem and caused it to stop functioning for a split second, bringing about the fainting spell. Why? Because it was information that was not subject to an analysis by the neocortex and went straight to the brain stem.

Here is a true story, reported in Korean newspapers in the mid-seventies. A mother whose little child had somehow slipped into a tiger's cage bent the metal bars of the cage apart with bare hands and rescued the child. Afterwards, she couldn't move the bars even a millimeter, despite using all her strength. How did this happen? Where did such strength come from? It came from the power of her brain stem, activated when the information that her child was in mortal danger was registered with purity and urgency, and not filtered through the neocortex. This is the same type of extraordinary powers we read about in the Bible when a cripple suddenly walks and an incurably sick child wakes up smiling at a word from Jesus. The total belief in Jesus' healing powers and divinity, registered by the brain stem directly, brought about such a miracle. Peter walking on water is another example.

Did you know that if you truly believe that an ordinary coin is scalding hot, you will raise a blister on the spot in your hand where that coin is placed? That's because you believe it without undue analysis. How about the story of a paralyzed man jumping up and running from a room when a large serpent suddenly appeared out of nowhere? How can such things happen? Because the fantastic reservoir of power in your brain stem has been accessed. The reality of life, miraculous abilities, and surreal powers can be found in the brain stem. Imagine what would happen if we could use the power of the brain stem for our spiritual advancement for the betterment of humankind? That's the goal of Brain Respiration, for inside the brain stem lies the key to raising our spiritual awareness and meeting the Creator Within. Even the most accomplished academician cannot mature spiritually through his or her neo-cortex alone. Reason and logic can do nothing to satisfy our basic spiritual needs. The key is in harnessing the power of the brain stem.

Enlightenment as a Physiological Phenomenon

So, how is the three-layer structure of our brain related to our spiritual advancement? Simple. Many people have vague and mystical ideas about enlightenment and divinity. But so-called enlightenment, if expressed in neurophysiological terms, means the reintegration of the triple layers of our brain. And all of us can achieve this enlightenment with proper training. It's akin to working out to slim down or to increase your muscle mass by a certain percentage. All you need is proper training, guidance from a gym trainer, and a sensible diet. I want to be clear on this: enlightenment is not some mystical experience available to only those who are chosen by some divine method. I want to strip away the mystical veil from enlightenment. Enlightenment is an experience available to everyone, should he or she make the choice to want to be enlightened. After all, you can't have a nice physical body if you don't work at it. This is the exact same thing. You have to train spiritually to reach, and keep yourself at, the level of enlightenment. And Brain Respiration is the training method presented by *Dahn Hak*.

Generally, our focus, our awareness, and our everyday concentration are located in the neocortex layer of our brains, with its reasoning and analyzing frame of mind. This is inevitable because this competition-driven society of ours forces us to use our neocortex constantly. To do better than the other students in class, we have to memorize. To earn more money and be promoted in the workplace, we have to constantly come up with new ideas and methods. In a competitive social paradigm, we cannot escape the realm of the neocortex. However, with such constant usage, the neocortex is under pressure always, leading to various stress-related ailments such as compulsive disorder and insomnia. In fact, a Duke University Medical School study in 1998 concluded that close to one hundred percent of modern ailments can be traced back to one factor: stress. We have lost our ability to relax.

It is the cerebral limbic system that demands that we fulfill its appetite for sex and food, in addition to satisfying its need for security, recognition, and dominance. We have been trying so far to appease our cerebral limbic system through competition. However the wants of the cerebral limbic system are endless and limitless in nature, always leaving something more to be desired. It is impossible to fully satisfy our cerebral limbic system unless we do it through the power of the brain stem. That is the crux of Brain Respiration.

Let's take love, for example. We all want to be loved. We fall into despairing loneliness if we cannot satisfy the need for love that originates from the cerebral limbic system. Up till now, the cerebral limbic system thought that love came from outside sources, from other people around us. However, love can also come from inside. The brain stem has the ability to create and manufacture limitless love, certainly enough to satisfy our greedy cerebral limbic system one hundred percent.

Love expresses itself in many ways. People laugh and cry because of love or lack thereof. Because we love, we hate, become jealous, and shed tears. Because the cerebral limbic system has so far been trying to satisfy its need for love through external factors, it may have sought love from someone with blond hair and tall. It may have wanted love only from those with a first-rate education and the right mix of humor and self-confidence. It wanted love only from the wealthy. It has been impossible to meet these conditions for love because the cerebral limbic system looked for love only from the outside. It wanted relative love, the "little" love that the outside provides.

Now the cerebral limbic system has heard that we are all One and that all life is interrelated. However, such information has made an impression upon the cerebral limbic system because the information was cold and dry, not accompanied by any experiential evidence such as happiness or love that would allow it to be permanently absorbed into the brain. When the cerebral limbic system truly "knows" that all is One and that True Love exists within us, we will find the absolute peace and happiness that we are looking for. To accomplish this, we need the power of the brain stem. Within our brain stem lies not only True Love but also true creativity of life. This is the place where we can find the Creator Within. We now know that the Creator Within has a specific address within our bodies.

Let us take a trip inside our brain stem. When your conscious awareness penetrates through the outer layers of the brain into the innermost one, you will feel a rapture such as you have never felt before. You will express that rapture through tears and smiles. You will feel the everlasting well-spring of life within you. Brain Respiration is designed to act as a travel guide to your own divinity within.

The purpose of Brain Respiration is to gently move our conscious awareness from our neocortex, where it is most of the time, through the cerebral limbic system and into the brain stem. Ultimately, we seek to control the power of the brain stem to meet with the Creator Within and raise our spiritual awareness.

To control the brain stem, the neocortex needs to be at rest. The neocortex is in a state of rest when we are asleep. However, our awareness is also asleep at the same time, making it impossible for us to consciously control the brain stem with a conscious awareness. Is it possible for our neocortex to be asleep and for our awareness be awake? Such a state is called "meditation."

Our brain emits four basic types of waves: beta, alpha, theta, and delta. When we are experiencing anger or hate, the frequency of our brain waves increases. Beta wave occurs during a state of emotional turmoil or excitement, leading to quick fatigue and listlessness. In a meditative state, the brain wave reaches the alpha stage, resembling sleep. However, just because you sit cross-legged and close your eyes doesn't mean that you are meditating. In fact, you might be bombarded with useless thoughts. The reason that it is very difficult for your awareness to sink lower into the inner layers of your brain is that the route is not open. There are guards at the gates leading into each inner layer of the brain. You need a secret password to enter. If there weren't any password, then everyone would have freely made the trip and be enlightened, holding conversations with the Creator Within at any time. Unfortunately, that is not so. Luckily, however, through Brain Respiration you can silence your neocortex, satisfy your cerebral limbic system, and steal into the brain stem to step into the place that goes beyond space and time into Creation itself. You will meet your Creator Within. You will meet *Yuln'yo*.

Let us take a trip together.

Ki Energy Sensitivity Training

Before we embark on the road to the brain stem, there is one prerequisite you have to master, and that is your sensitivity to the *Ki* energy. *Ki* energy is the life energy that animates us. It is the Cosmic Energy that fills the universe. It is within and around us. And only by riding upon the wave of this energy can we enter the brain stem. If you place yourself in the embrace of *Ki* energy, you naturally will your neocortex to stop its functions and rest. *Ki* energy can be divided into three types: heat, attraction, and electricity. It is well known that we have a low voltage running the length of our physical bodies. This is a manifestation of *Ki* energy.

Conquer your anxiety. Believe in the existence of your higher self. You can find your True Self only through peace of mind. What is easier, finding an object in a clean room or in a room cluttered with junk? This is where *Ki* energy can help you. Because we are such doubtful creatures, we do not believe until we can see, smell, hear, or touch something. This is exactly what you will do with your life energy. You will feel it, I promise. And when you feel it, you will believe. You will believe that maybe there is something in this world other than your immediate physical and mental surroundings. You will begin to ask the really important questions. You will sense a realm of possibility beyond what you are used to. You will find your spiritual potential. Grab on to it and ride it to your True Self. *Ki* energy will be the vehicle on which you will cross that bridge.

Let us all feel this *Ki* energy together. Hold your hands in front of you in a prayer position, with the palms facing each other. Do not touch, but leave at least two inches between your hands. Concentrate on your hands. Hands. Hands. Hands. Your concentration is like a ray of bright light. Feel the light illuminate your hands. You will feel a certain warmth in your hands, a certain tingling sensation, or even a feeling that a bug is crawling up and down your hands. This is *Ki* energy you feel. Let us now use the power of this force to push our hands apart.

Imagine that your hands are drifting apart. Concentrate on your hands with singular point of conscious light and will them to move apart. Even without conscious motor control, you will feel your hand somehow moving apart on their own accord. Now let's will them together. Closer, you think. Closer, closer, closer. Soon, your hands will drift back together again. You have just learned the basic concept of *Ki* energy and your will. Wherever you direct your will, the energy follows. What a powerful law of nature this is.

Now try creating a ball of energy with your mind. Imagine that you are holding a bright ball of light in your hands. Feel the texture of this ball, its contours, and its perfectly round shape. Make it grow and make it shrink. Play around with it gently, never letting the sensation disappear. You have just made this energy through nothing more than the power of your mind. You willed it, and the surrounding energy came together to form a ball. Be in awe of the power of your mind.

Take a Trip into the Brain Stem through Vibration

All life is in constant motion. Even rocks and mountains are in constant vibration. Every existence is dancing to the rhythm of the Cosmic Order. Life celebrates itself through constant vibration. And through vibration we can enter into the brain stem. You will experience the reality of your life in your brain stem.

Place your hands, palms up, on your knees. Focus the light of your awareness onto your hands. Hands, hands, and hands. Imagine that heavy rocks are weighing down your hands in place. Silently count to one and raise your hands to your chest, only to let them sink to your knees with a silent two. One, up. Two, down. And repeat. Only through simple, repetitive movements will you allow your neocortex to momentarily stop. Now completely relax your shoulders and feel the heaviness of your hands as they lie on your knees. Feel them getting heavier until they are completely attached to the knees.

You are now in complete relaxation and comfort. In this relaxed state, just concentrate on your breathing only. You feel your neocortex go silent and sense the restlessness of the cerebral limbic system. Your awareness is now at this layer. The cerebral limbic system is gently shaking in the flow of the vibration that is emitted by the brain stem. You can now feel with an immediacy you have not felt before the myriad emotions that have been locked into the cerebral limbic system. Let them out now. All the loneliness, hurt, and sorrows. Let them all out right now. Let the tears flow if they will, for through the tears the cerebral limbic system is being cleansed.

Breathe in . . . and out.

Now your awareness is in the cerebral limbic system. A little more, and you can enter the brain stem. Inside the brain stem you will feel an incredible rush of joy and happiness. Prepare to enter the brain stem. Entrust yourself to the life force that is working through you. Feel the subtle vibration of life that radiates outward from the brain stem. A soft, subtle vibration. Feel it cross your chest into your shoulders and arms. Vibration is life. Feel the vibration travel up and down your spine. Feel its power getting stronger, moving your body from side to side and front to back. Feel it shake you with the power of life itself. Everyone is in constant vibration. It is only that you don't recognize and acknowledge it. Your heartbeat is a form of vibration. Contraction and relaxation. Expansion and contraction. Let it sing the song of life within you. Inside the vibration is the absolute joy and peace. Inside the vibration is the True Love of the cosmos. Through vibration you are becoming One with the Creator.

Within your brain stem lies the direct route to all life. Your awareness is now at the doorstep of the brain stem. You feel the power of its vibration with your whole being. You feel its golden aura of life. Inside the golden aura, you feel the constant rush of vibration as it pulsates with the Cosmic Rhythm. Listen as the brain stem speaks to you. Obey as it invites you to approach and speak with the Creator Within. Feel in awe at the preciousness of the moment and be glad of the love that you feel emanating from the brain stem like brilliant rays of light and know that you are becoming One with the divinity that you possess inside. Feel Heaven, Earth, and human come together in this moment. Experience the benevolent patience and love of the cosmos as it showers you with an absolute, divine love. That is the Creator Within. That is the *Yuln'yo*. Shake at the pounding waves of warm energy as they sweep through your consciousness. You can feel all this through vibration as you ride upon the crest of your own energy.

The actual Brain Respiration program consists of five levels. The first level is Brain Sensitizing, during which you will learn to heighten the brain's sensitivity to *Ki* energy. The second level is Brain Softening, through which you will learn to truly relax your brain. The third is Brain Cleaning, in which you will learn to let go of pent-up or bad emotions and release the associated negative energy. The fourth level is Brain Reinforming, through which you will control the flow and the quality of information being input into our brains. The last level is Brain Energizing, by which you will selectively and purposely select the type of information and functions that will allow you to effect a spiritual uplift and contribute positively in the process. And it is riding on the vibration of your own *Ki* energy that you will master these levels.

Through vibration you can reexperience the Cosmic Lifeline. Through vibration you can feel the power of your brain stem. Through vibration you will be capable of amazing healing powers. You will experience the perfectness of life through vibration. You will hear the Creator Within through this vibration of life.

Individual Enlightenment

Enlightenment is choice.
Enlightenment is courage.
Enlightenment is finding your True Self.
Enlightenment is recovering True Love.
Enlightenment is celebrating the *Yuln'yo* in your heart.
Enlightenment is a goal you can reach through training.

Enlightenment is all these and more. And all these and more can be achieved by letting your awareness take a trip down to your brain stem, in which lies the seat of the Creator Within and the direct route to the Cosmic Order. We are no longer in an age in which we can easily go off into the mountains for spiritual training or meditation. It is true that some yogis and monks, and even a few "regular" people are able to do exactly that, living a life of ascetic simpleness and hardship, perhaps even finding enlightenment at the end. For the majority of us, however, such a life is simply impossible. We need a realistic and everyday form of spiritual training to help us find the answers to life's ultimate questions. And that is the role that Brain Respiration seeks to fill.

With Brain Respiration, we can ride upon waves of energy vibration and embark on a spiritual adventure to find our True Selves. Simply put, Brain Respiration is the Way to Enlightenment for the Everyman. Yet, as I mentioned before, individual enlightenment that does not make a concrete difference in society is no enlightenment at all. We are not looking for just one more enlightened being to walk among us. We are all looking to be enlightened beings ourselves. To that end, we need to form a society of New Humans, whose goal will be to effect a total transformation of the human spirit, and to collectively recover our sense of True Love.

A Personal Story— The Death of a Friend

When I was twelve, I asked a close friend to go swimming with me in a lake. Although he didn't want to, I convinced him anyway. So, we were swimming when he drowned. I almost drowned myself trying to get him ashore. Then what could I do? I didn't even know CPR then. So, I carried his lifeless body back to his house, almost four miles, and placed it in the yard. His parents went crazy with shock and grief, and if the neighbors hadn't stopped him, my friend's father would have beaten me to death right then and there.

But by then I was already beyond caring. I was only thinking about death. So this is how people die. So this is what death feels like. I became obsessed with death. For the next six months, I was an emotional mess of guilt, fear, and morbid curiosity. I became a sort of an anarchistic, cynical atheist. All the teachers in my school and my parents were up in arms about me because after I talked to any classmate, he would become just like me—depressed, angry, and lost, not a bit interested in school work. I would ask them, "Why do you study?" and grill them until they admitted that they knew nothing about what life was. "You could die the next day. What possible good could studying do you?"

It got to the point that I thought about death all the time. I carried around some sleeping pills with me because I wanted to feel some power or control over my own death. I didn't want death to sneak up on me. So, I decided to die. I went to a remote place where I could watch the stars, and dug up a deep hole in which I could lie down. Then I gulped down some liquor along with the sleeping pills and waited for death to take me as I watched the twinkling stars. Then this person came to rescue me. This mother of a local postman. She said later that somebody came to her in a dream telling her to save this person who is trying to commit suicide in an abandoned lot.

She somehow got me out of the hole and took me to nearby Kwon Hospital. The doctor there worked all night to save me. The first thing that I did upon becoming conscious again was to curse at the doctor for saving me. I told him that I wanted to die and why did he interfere? He slapped me across the face. He yelled at me to go ahead and die and he wouldn't save me this time. Afterwards, I felt sorry and relieved at the same time. It was then I realized that death is not something you can wish or not wish upon yourself. But I still hadn't realized what life was all about. I was only in my early twenties when I came across something that allowed me to feel the *Ki* again. And through *Ki*, my True Self.

Group Enlightenment— New Human Society

It Has Already Existed

When you imagine and preach a spiritual utopia, you run into a wall of opposition that consists of cynics and skeptics who say that such a thing has never been done before and will never be achieved. When I hear such doubts, I don't have to fight an abstract with an abstract. I just point to history and let them judge for themselves, for there was a world once in which enlightened beings lived in utter harmony and peace. Let me briefly touch upon that story.

The story comes from an ancient historical text called *Pu Do Chi*, describing the creation of the world and the early history of humankind. The book starts out with, "In the beginning, there was a Word." Familiar? And the word is *Yuln'yo*. The book defines *Yuln'yo* as the Creator of all things. It says, "Stars came out *Yuln'yo* as it circled and rebirthed countlessly, sending forth music and rhythms of life, giving rise to Margo and the Great Castle of Margo." *Yuln'yo,* as defined in this ancient Creation text, is the direct expression of the will of the Creator, a basic rhythm of light, sound, and vibration that forms the underpinnings of all existence. We human beings are made up of this *Yuln'yo,* according to this.

Then, what is this Margo and the Castle of Margo that *Yuln'yo* gave rise to? They are the original world that consisted of enlightened beings living in harmony. This is the world that we seek to go back to at our deepest spiritual levels.

The book tells us that this celestial being called Margo, born out of *Yuln'yo,* gave birth to two daughters, without any need for a partner since she was complete unto herself. These two daughters, being also complete in their femaleness and maleness, gave birth to two males and two females each. Therefore, we have eight beings, four sons and four daughters, giving us four couples. These were the "Yellow Couple," the "White Couple," the "Black Couple," and the "Blue Couple"—giving us hints of racial diversification in the very beginning of history, with a clear route to a common ancestor. The only food available was the "milk from the ground."

Then the rhythm of *Yuln'yo* was once again called into play by Margo to create the Heavens and the Earth and the water and the *Ki* energy in complete harmony. The four couples each took responsibility for a different aspect of the Earth. The Yellows were put in charge of the Earth, the Whites in charge of *Ki* energy, the Blacks in charge of fire, and the Blues in charge of water. And in order to create life to live on Earth, Margo commanded the four couples to open up their ribs to give birth. Each couple gave birth to three sons and three daughters, for a total of twenty-four children. After a few generations, the twenty-four became three thousand and then twelve thousand, who all lived in Margo's Castle in total harmony, all drinking the milk of the Earth. They were gentle of nature, pure of energy, heard the music of the heavens always, could walk and run freely, could turn into a golden light when their work on Earth was done, could communicate without speaking, could disappear into the light, and lived long lives because their energy was One with the Heaven and Earth. In short, it was a perfect world. Until the big downfall.

As the people became more numerous, the need to wait for the nourishing milk of the Earth became acute, and some started feeling hunger. One of them, unable to stand the hunger, ate a grape and started the humans on a slippery downward slope. The book calls this the "Downfall of the Five Tastes," because the grape has five different tastes to it:

bitterness, sourness, sweetness, saltiness, and tanginess. By eating grapes, human beings lost their world of absolute Oneness and developed the ability to differentiate and judge. They saw the difference between good and evil, cleanness and dirt, and Heaven and Earth. They differentiated between their physical, energy, and spiritual bodies. They lost their ability to commune directly with the *Yuln'yo* and thereby lost their sense of Oneness with all.

In this story, the original couples—Yellows, Whites, Blacks, and Blues—take collective responsibility and decide to leave the castle with all their descendants, for they have decided they could not stay in that perfect world in such an imperfect state. Outside the castle, they go on their separate ways. Before leaving, however, they vow to recover their divine selves and return to the castle, taking with them two things each that will help them accomplish this: one, a method to control and commune with the *Ki* energy that forms the source of all things visible and invisible; and two, a simple scripture of eighty-one letters summarizing the essential Truths of the cosmos. This scripture is called the "Heavenly Code." It is our great fortune that we have this scripture with us still. Then the couples go in separate directions, promising to meet inside the castle walls again.

This history of Margo's Castle shares many things with Genesis and other Creation stories. The similarities are obvious. It speaks to the fact that we, as humanity, share the common root that we all have a deep spiritual need to go back to. But in order to go back, we need to recover the sense of Oneness and harmony that we have lost. And we can recover this sense by achieving enlightenment, for enlightenment is our natural, truly original state of being. When enough people recover this Oneness, when enough people reach enlightenment, we will march together back to Margo's castle and collectively shout for our ultimate Grandma to let us back in. I bet that she's waiting for us with all her heart.

What a welcome party it will be.

It Is the Humans Who
Have to Do the Work

Why do humans insist upon differentiating everything, ever since we ate of the grape in Margo's Castle, or the forbidden fruit in the Garden of Eden? Why do we separate God from humans? Mine from yours? My religion from your religion? My country from your country? Is it so difficult to create this concept of "us" as you and I as One? Can we open up our minds a little bit more to allow the possibility of coexistence in harmony and tolerance? Can we create this new road, the road that the Creator surely would want us to take? The road we are on right now will ultimately lead us to ruination.

Looking back on our various traditions and history, we know that, although the Creator has given us life, He has also given us free will. The Creator has given us the power to utilize nature for our benefits but has not actively stopped our abuses, giving us choice in our actions. The world's problems lie not in the realm of the Creator, but in the realm of humans. If humanity should perish due to our misjudgments and arrogance, the Creator will watch and observe but will not actively intervene, for He has given us all the tools necessary to make corrections. It is up to us to do the work. The Creator is not here so that we may shift our responsibility over. We have to take responsibility as individuals, as a society, and as a world.

We can no longer be satisfied with praying alone. The Creator gives us a message but will not take the leading role in changing this world. No lightning bolts will fly out of the blue and strike down all the mass murderers in the world as examples of punishment to all evildoers. No wars will stop because an image of Jesus, made up of clouds, will look down upon a battlefield. It is up to us humans. We can make ourselves miserable or happy. We can destroy or save this Earth. Do not make the mistake of thinking that the Creator will save this world at the last moment. The Creator did not make this world sick and will not make this world better. The Creator just makes sure that our hearts keep beating and the Earth keeps spinning. The Creators created us to do the rest. We are the Creator, creating as us.

The future is in our collective hands. We need to awaken that part of the Creator that we have within us and really wish for a world of happiness and harmony for all humankind. As we have made a choice to be enlightened, we have to make a collective choice to do so as well. We need a collective choice and collective courage. This work can't be done by one or two people alone. This work has to be done by millions upon millions of people.

I propose that in ten years, we reach a threshold of one hundred million spiritually enlightened humans around the world who can act as catalysts to effect a worldwide Enlightenment Revolution. I view this initial one hundred million as the critical mass we need to ignite the fire. When these one hundred million people make the choice to reach a collective enlightenment, then we will change the destiny of the Earth itself. The healing vibration of their choices and determination will cure the Earth of the ills that we have caused. Then we will finally be on our way to Margo's Castle again.

Hello, Grandma!

What Is a New Human?

In order to create a New Human Society, we need New Humans. One hundred million in ten years, to be exact, in order to reach the critical mass for the Enlightenment Revolution. So what is a New Human?

A New Human is someone who has met with the *Yuln'yo* within him or her. The Creator Within. When *Yuln'yo* is expressed as powerful creativity and vision, when the Creator Within is expressed as rich emotions and loving warmth, only then can a person reach a state in which he or she can see everyone as separate flowers blossoming from a single tree. Physiologically, this means the reintegration of the three layers of the brain: the basic life-giving power of the brain stem, the emotions of the limbic system, and the creativity of the neocortex all rolled into one.

More systemically, there are five conditions to being a New Human:

One, a New Human needs to be healthy. So far we have defined health only in the physical sense. Lack of disease was considered healthy. New Human health is defined as the state in which a person can use one hundred percent of his or her energy and abilities according to the way that was intended. This is the essence of "my body is not me, but mine." A healthy person is someone who is truly the master of his or her own body.

Two, a New Human needs to be intelligent. A New Human needs to use his or her intelligence the way he or she intends. "My mind is mine, not me." Intelligence here means not the ability to process complicated information but the ability to create positive, healthy, and true information that is helpful to those who absorb it. Intelligence is a matter of problem-solving ability and requires as preconditions deep insight and discipline.

Three, a New Human needs to be emotionally rich. He or she needs to feel the beauty of existence and harmony. This does not mean that you should be fickle or emotionally undulating. Nor does this mean that you should avoid emotional swings by being barren of emotions themselves. A New Human knows how to use emotions to appreciate the surrounding beauty, making life rich, harmonious, and relaxing. Our emotions are not us, just tools for us to "feel" the Truths about life.

Four, a New Human needs to be honest and conscientious. The line between wrong or right can vary according to culture and age, but the will to be honest and conscientious is always forever and uniformly valued in all cultures and throughout history. Conscientiousness means listening to the voice of divinity within. Without this, it is impossible to be healthy in body and mind. Who am I? What is the purpose of my life? Conscientiousness is the will to listen to the answers to these questions honestly and courageously.

Five, a New Human is a divine person. Divinity is an expression of energy that connects us to the Cosmic Energy. When we are inspired, we are connected. Everything in this universe is filled with this divine energy, and therefore, all existence is divine. It is up to the individual to decide upon what level of divinity he or she chooses to experience and stay at. We have access to all types of information, messages, and ideas, but it is our choice to accept which ones. I propose that a New Human is someone who uses the divinity within as the filter through which he or she culls through the information that is input into the brain. And experiencing and recalling forth this divinity needs to become an everyday habit, not just a temporary ray of light that is soon lost.

A New Human is someone who has made enlightenment a habit and trains hard to keep up the level of his or her spiritual fitness. As I said, we need one hundred million New Humans in ten years to reach a critical mass that will jump start the Enlightenment Revolution.

Let us join in.

A True Democracy

Human beings are born into a system called "society" in which they are educated and expected to live according to certain norms of behavior. However, this system has become twisted in such a way that it recognizes only the number ones, and will neither acknowledge nor reward anyone else. This system has become twisted in such a way that a dictator or an organization is able to decide for us what we must do to gain our sense of self-worth. This system is definitely twisted in such a way that our politics, economy, religion, science, and education have been used to advance the self-centered and narrow goals of a particular individual, group, nation, and others instead of being used to achieve human harmony and peace. We human beings are like puppets dancing on a stage, unable to look beyond the curtains and realize that we are not dancing to the rhythm of the divine music that's playing in the theater.

Can we truly let the appetites of the few dictate the future of the world? Do we all want this? If we go on our present way, the elite few who lead this system will themselves be left out in the dust as the self-destructive system of constant competition drives the Earth into destruction. One or two enlightened people cannot stop this machine. Twelve disciples cannot help us now. We need one hundred million enlightened disciples. It is up to us, as individuals, as a society, as humanity, to change the course upon which we have embarked.

In his historic Gettysburg Address, President Lincoln spoke of a government of the people, by the people, and for the people. Close to 150 years later, the seed of democracy has been planted throughout the world and is blossoming forth, having been judged by society as being superior to socialism. Democracy is gaining stature as the ideal form of government. However, although we see the roots and the stems of democracy all around the world, in no country has the flower of democracy bloomed in full yet.

What is true democracy? I want to call it the *"Hong-Ik* Democracy," or Wide-Benefits Democracy. A democracy not for the advancement of the elite few, but for the betterment of the whole society. A democracy in which politics, economy, religion, culture, and science can be used for the benefit of all its participants and users, with the sole common purpose being the betterment of all of us, not at the expense of others, but in conjunction with others, until there is no "Other." A true democracy is not for the dominators or the conquerors, but for those who seek to share.

We cannot create such a system with more legislation or regulations. We can create such a system only when our collective human consciousness has reached a certain level of spiritual awakening. Then such a system will arise. It will virtually create itself.

I truly give my respect and utmost praise to those who have advanced democracy to where it is now, for without their Herculean efforts, we could not have realized the material and mental advances that make possible the spiritual advance that is our next step as humanity: to create a true, spiritual democracy. What the people want, the people will get. And it is up to the people of the United States, as the cradle of democracy in the world, to lead us all to that next level of democracy by using her reach and power and status, creating a truly beautiful world. Maybe this is the purpose for which the United States was born.

The Earth may look large, but it has truly become a small town through advances in communications and transportation.

That's why we call it an Earth Village. If we gather our strengths together, can we not positively influence this little village? What are the obstacles that face us? Not enough food? No. Environmental problems? Since we human beings are the cause of the environmental problems that we face today, we can also be the solution. We just need a shift in our thinking. We just need to move away from the paradigm of competition and domination. Then this world will not end. In fact, the world will prosper and return to its original place as the warm cradle of self-discovery and the advancement of human spirituality. And such a world is true democracy.

A Personal Story—Waking the Power of *Ki* Within

The first time I felt the power of *Ki* energy was when I went on an errand for my mother when I was five. The next time was in my mid-twenties, when I visited an old bookstore in the old center of Seoul in Korea. I picked up a book whose cover was falling off and turned it to the first page. There I saw a sentence that sent jolts of electricity running through me. It said, "If you achieve enlightenment through positive energy and deeds, you will be invincible." As soon as I read that sentence, a live wire was running through me and an invisible warmth formed a blanket around me. I was a third-degree black belt in Tae Kwon Do and had even run a martial arts school, but I had never felt this way before. I did not want to let this feeling go. As I rode the bus back home, I sat huddled to myself, quiet, drunk on that wonderful and powerful feeling. Afterwards, my life became dictated by *Ki* energy.

The next day, I woke up at four o'clock in the morning. And the morning after that. And the morning after that. Later on, I found out that four A.M. is the time when the energy connection between the cosmos and Earth is the strongest. If you become sensitized to the flow of *Ki,* then your body will naturally respond to its rhythm. I did not used to be a morning person at all. But afterwards, I would get up at four A.M.

without alarms or prompting. I would get up and climb up a hill behind where I lived and train and meditate for hours, without regard to time. I would practice *Dahn Jon* breathing in order to feel and control the flow of *Ki* energy throughout my body and mind.

What is *Dahn Jon* breathing? It is a system of exercise and breathing techniques designed to sensitize you to the flow of *Ki* to eventually allow you to control and utilize the energy for various purposes. *Dahn Jon* is a point in your lower belly, about two inches from your navel, that acts as an energy gathering place. Basically, it is a portal to the world of energy. Knowledge of it goes back into the mist of Asian civilization. It is this *Dahn Jon* breathing technique that I have modernized and organized into specific steps and made available for everyone to try. I started my first Dahn Center in 1985, and now we have over three hundred centers in Korea and over fifty in the United States. *Dahn Jon* breathing should be your first conscious step into the realm of *Ki* energy.

I practiced and trained until I achieved a certain level in *Ki* training. In the throes of *Ki* energy, I was able to pull up the roots of trees, experience every single bone in my body disintegrate and reintegrate again, and felt my whole body shake violently as the *Ki* energy coursed through my body. Also, I was able to see and talk to the spirits or ghosts. I would call and send away different spirits. I would see ghosts haunting or attaching themselves to some house or person. I would talk to these ghosts and tell them to leave. I was also able to sense the different diseases or states of mind of different people before even talking to them. A person with cancer feels and smells differently from a healthy person. A person with diabetes is the same way. A person who just went through an emotional trauma has a different feel to him or her. Their energy vibration is just different. Local Mudangs, or traditional Korean shamans, would come to me with their heads bowed and want me to lead them in some exorcism or another. They would prepare pork heads and other required foods and dance crazily for hours, banging on their drums and wailing and chanting. And I would see these spirits hanging around, some with hate and vengeance from previous lifetimes, and I would tell them, "Stop it already. You are only increasing your own Karma debt, no matter what manners of wrongs this person's ancestors have done to you." Then they would go. Once you enter into the world of energy, it is no big deal. What are ghosts anyway? Just a pale reflection of energy that is too weak to manifest physically.

One morning when it was bitterly cold out, I was sitting in the middle of fresh snow, meditating. This was the last day of a hundred straight days of training that I promised myself. If I didn't finish out today, then I would have failed. The ninety-nine days before would have been for naught. With that in mind, I sat like a stone statute in the middle of a snow-covered field, braving the skin-biting wind. I think it was about minus twenty degrees Celsius. I had trained before in weather about minus ten degrees, and was able to fight off the cold by accumulating and directing the flow of energy around me. But this was severe cold. My body shook and my breathing became haggard.

I just accepted the cold. I wanted to wait it out. I would watch what this extreme cold was doing to my body. I said to myself, "Let's see how cold it really gets and what it does to me." After a short while, my body started going numb. After that, my breathing became even more difficult. I was losing consciousness, slipping into a warm haze. I wanted to get up at that time, but I couldn't. My body was no longer mine to command. It was too late. I was going to freeze to death right there. So, I gave up.

I mean, really gave up. I didn't give up just in words, thoughts, or mind even, but totally. I gave myself up in absolute completeness to God above to do as He wished. God is not stupid. God doesn't get suckered into helping you because you say that you will do something. God knows when you mean something with your whole being. So, when I felt my death coming, I gave up every attachment I had and trusted God to do with me as He saw fit. I gave myself up completely and trusted with absolute trust. "Please take me, for I trust you to do the best for me."

It was at this moment that my *Dahn Jon* point in my lower belly started coming alive and spewing out furious heat, melting all the snow around me. I felt a powerful stream of *Ki* energy course through my body and give it life again, forming a capsule of energy barrier that protected me. This wasn't something that I could have done. This was my innermost life energy coming alive in the moment of utmost urgency and complete trust.

I learned a profound lesson through this episode: that you need divine help, there is a divine connection to assist you in this journey. And how do you access this power? Complete belief and trust. Give yourself up completely to the trust of the beneficence of the divine.

So, through *Ki* training, I was able to see spirits, diagnose people without touching, sheath myself in a protective capsule of energy, manifest incredible physical strengths, and do other "miraculous" things. But I still couldn't answer the simple question: Why was I born? Without the answer to this question, I would remain someone who could play around with energy, a mere technician. Nothing more. And what good is that? What good is knowing how to uproot trees without knowing what to use this power for? I was reminded of a story I had heard about Lao Tzu, the founder of Taoism. He had a bright student who trained for ten years in order to be able to control the flow of *Ki* energy to such an extent that he could form an energy bridge over a nearby river. One day, he showed Lao Tzu what he could do and walked across the river on the invisible energy bridge, back and forth. Expecting high praise, the student was flabbergasted when Lao Tzu turned purple with anger and shouted at him at the top of his voice, "You stupid idiot. You spent ten years to do a stupid trick when, all this time, there was a cheap ferry to get you across the river at any time you wished!"

That's exactly how I felt. Like the student. I was nothing more than a show pony.

I wanted the ultimate answers and not cheap thrills.

Human Enlightenment— A Spiritual-Cultural Movement

All We Have to Do Is
Play Well with Each Other

People often ask me, "What can we do to solve the world's problems?"

Whenever people ask me those questions, I am reminded of the time I met VIPs from the United Nations. My guide at that time, to my great surprise and chagrin, introduced me as the "spiritual leader of the Orient of the type that only comes along once every century." After such a hyperbolic introduction, I was immediately met with the question, "How can we solve the problem of religious wars in this world?" Then another question was thrown at me without giving me a chance to respond. "What can we do to solve the world's racial conflicts?" Other questions about the environment, education, poverty, and drugs followed. "Is sex really a sin or is it okay?" another asked.

The fact was that these people who were asking me these questions were themselves experts in their respective fields. They knew more about the concrete aspects of these problems that they have asked about than I could ever learn in my lifetime, since they had just been discussing them without results in the UN before I came. With a wise and sublime look on my face, for I had to look the role that my introduction had just given me, I told them the answer was simple. Then they all looked shocked and waited eagerly for the answer.

I told them, "All we have to do is play well with each other. All the problems we face now in this world came about because we, as human beings, could not play well with each other. We don't play well with ourselves, first of all. Second, we don't play well with other humans. Third, we don't play well with other groups. Fourth, nations don't play well with other nations. Fifth, races don't play well with each other. Nor do religions play well with each other. We don't even play well with the environment. And do you know why we don't play well? Because we have never been taught to how to play well. Our education so far has taught us to differentiate, to compete, to create rivals. If we play well with nature, our environmental problems will be gone. If we play well with other human beings, the difference between the haves and the have nots will disappear. If religions play well with one another, then religious wars will end. If races play well with each other, racism will be a thing of the past. Playing well is the solution."

And this is truly what I think the solution is. So far, the information in our brains has misled us into competing against one another. We are being controlled by these types of information, instead of controlling them. If we as individuals can train ourselves to control and detach ourselves from the type of information that forces us to always compete, if we process our information better through our divine filter, if we use our brains the way they are intended to be used, then the problems will just disappear. Because we will have made a conscious choice to be enlightened. Because we will have set into motion the Spiritual-Cultural Movement that will teach us all how to play well with one another.

Change the Brain, Change the World

Within us, and filling our every living moment, are constant vibrations of life. In our hearts, brains, and bodies we can feel the rhythmic pounding that echoes the Cosmic Rhythm of the universe. All we have to do is to grab on to these vibrations and let them echo throughout the world, breaking through the barriers that seek to prevent us from hearing the beautiful melody.

"Change the Brain, Change the World." This can be the message that will lead us to create the culture and society that can take us into the twenty-first century. By controlling the information that is input into your brain, you will regain your physical, mental, and spiritual health, become a healer, and join other healers in curing this Earth of her ills.

In political terms, we have to effect a true democracy, whose goal is the betterment of all people, not just the elitist few. We can no longer maintain the present relationship between the governors and the governed, but must create a new relationship of common respect and love. We need a *Hong-Ik* Democracy. A Wide-Benefits Democracy.

In religious terms, we have to move away from the doctrine of an external, arbitrary God and move into the world of divinity within, not just as an object of worship but as an active divinity which we can use to change the world. We should no longer passively worship the divine, but actively use the divine to create a better world. We need to become enlightenment activists. This is the essence of the Enlightenment Revolution: to become spiritual activists. To further this end, religions must rise out of the competition paradigm to which they have been slaves and truly work to raise the collective spiritual consciousness of the human race.

The purpose of the economy cannot be to serve egotistic ends, or to earn the most money with the least effort, or to squeeze out a higher working efficiency in the market place, or to create a higher abstract value for the various industries. The purpose of the economy should be to serve as a tool with which to help human beings on their journey of spiritual growth. We need a fundamental shift in direction from materialistic goals, with their basis in our physical selves, to spiritual goals, with their basis in our True Selves. The economy has to be just another tool in the toolbox helping us to fulfill our true purpose in life.

The same goes for science. Cloning, artificial intelligence, and other research is once again calling into question the exact definition of a human being. This question arises because we still think of ourselves only as physical beings. The definition of a human being must consist of our spiritual nature. So far, science has been used mainly to satisfy the appetite for control and domination of the few. So far, science has sometimes been used to rob us of our spiritual nature. Now science has to work to create concrete and materialistic underpinnings to help human beings achieve spiritual advancement on a global scale. The time has come to use science for spiritual means, for now it has given us the ability to germinate the seed of spiritual enlightenment throughout the world instantly and continuously.

Medicine needs to develop into a comprehensive field in which it not only treats physical diseases and pains but also treats the emotional, mental, and spiritual causes of the various ailments that make us suffer so. Medicine should seek to help people recover the natural harmony and balance of the body, mind, and spirit, and should act to prevent the physical manifestations of these essentially spiritual diseases, not "cure" them with purely physical means.

Education will become the most important field in all of the social sciences in the coming century, because ultimately it will be through education that people will learn to play with each other well. We must break out of the educational frame that only stresses egotism and competition, and create a new educational paradigm that teaches human worth, life's purpose, and the power of the brain to open up and expand the spiritual frontier on our cosmic journey. It will be through education that we'll create one hundred million New Humans in ten years and jump start the new Enlightenment Revolution.

Sports and arts should not strive to create only the few superstars and make them into idols of worship for purely economic purposes. Sports and arts should be just another one of the many ways through which humans can express their spiritual nature. They should become the means, not the ends, of spiritual journey and maturity.

All of the above are not something to be accomplished by experts. They can be achieved only if you have the sincerity and the purity in your purpose to recover your own divinity and collectively experience the spiritual awakening that is the destiny of humankind. It's almost as easy as drinking a glass of water. It's almost as easy as breathing the air. Its easiness has just been hidden under the complex twists and mazes that we have built over it.

I am not enough of an expert in each of the fields above to do more than just suggest directions toward which they should go. I don't have any special abilities or intelligence. However, one doesn't need special abilities or intelligence to make changes in this world. With personal choice and the discipline to train yourself spiritually, enlightenment is just a mere recovery of what you already have, a reminder of your True Self. Anyone can reach enlightenment. You only have to choose to. And you will not be required to make great self-sacrifices. You can truly kill two birds with one divine stone.

I write this book to ask all of you "anyones" to make the Enlightenment Revolution a reality. I want all of you to become experts in enlightenment. I want to see all of you in a new Earth Village that is full of love, peace, and most of all, harmony. In ten years. One hundred million of us.

A Personal Story—Twenty-one
Sleepless Days and Nights

After bemoaning the fact that I was just a simple *Ki* energy technician, I went back into the mountain and vowed to never come out until I had the answers to the questions that I was looking for. I chose to test the limits of my physical and mental endurance by not sleeping for twenty-one days straight. Ah, the torture I put myself through . . .

I tried everything not to sleep, including sitting at the edge of a sharp cliff and wrapping my arms around a thick branch of a tree so that the fear of falling down would keep me awake. I think I pulled many clumps of hair out during that period. After a week or so of no sleep, a severe headache of the magnitude that I have never felt came over me. It had been building for a while, but it struck with full force after a week or so. Pain accumulated in my eye sockets and my ears until I couldn't see or hear. As time went on, my brain seemed to shrivel up inside and start to desiccate. At the same time, my head seemed always on the verge of exploding. I knew that I would die soon. This was after about two weeks. I even received a fleeting temptation to sleep, drink, and even eat something in order to prolong my life a bit. I would have succumbed to that temptation had I not survived the training ordeal in the snow-covered field on that freezing day before.

The pain had gotten so bad that I knew I was beyond saving at this point. I just couldn't stand the pain anymore, but I comforted and strengthened my will by telling myself that "my body is mine, not me." This naturally translated into my brain being mine, not me. Therefore, it was only my brain hurting so badly, not me. So, if I left my body, then I would no longer feel such literally blinding and deafening pain. Boom! At the exact moment that thought crossed my mind, I found myself beyond my body, free of pain and in full clarity. With the loud boom, I felt the world open up before me, and an extremely soothing and refreshing feeling of cool warmth enveloped me.

In this incredible expanse of feelings, I heard a voice from the Heavens cry out, "Who am I!" Then the answer came, "I am the Cosmic Energy . . ." before my tongue started moving on its own and mouthing the phrase, "My energy is the Cosmic Energy, my mind is the Cosmic Mind." And vice versa. At this moment, I heard, with a profoundness that I cannot describe, the sound of the universe breathing. It was the sound of my own breathing. The universe and I are not separate. Nature and I are One. I can be the stars, the Moon, and the Sun. When you see other people, you see the connections that they all possess through the Cosmic Energy. This is so, and I hadn't realized it before.

I was beyond pain at that point of clarity, for I had no senses that I could feel. I was beyond my physical body. I had no fear because I had no senses. Without physical senses, you have no fear of pain, for you know you cannot feel physical pain. It's like escaping from a huge prison.

Then you realize that the door was open all the time. Then you feel foolish that you busted your head and bruised your body to squeeze yourself through the narrow bars of the prison when the door right next to the bars was ajar all the time. You can see the open door now that you are outside, now that your point of view has changed. That's why I say that enlightenment is such an obvious thing. All you have to do is step through the door. All it takes is your choice to will your feet to take you through the door that is open already!

However, as easy as it might be, enlightenment embodies all the life force and love of the universe, giving you the ability to save the whole human race with your one choice. Inside your heart lies True Love. Inside your heart lies Infinite Life. Inside your heart lies the Creator Within. When you realize this, the actualization and expression of your divinity becomes of the utmost importance, for passive and idle enlightenment is no enlightenment at all. At the moment of enlightenment, your number one goal should be to devise ways through which you can point out the open door to your fellow human beings. That is the true meaning of enlightenment. Sharing it.

Let us start an Enlightenment Revolution.

Index

About
the Author

Dr. Seung Heun Lee is the founder of the modern *Dahn Hak* Movement, a traditional Korean system of physical and mental exercises that seeks to use the energy, or *"Ki,"* system of the body to attain a spiritual awakening. Currently, *Dahn Hak* is a rapidly growing movement with more than three million participants worldwide; with three hundred centers in Korea, and fifty centers in the USA.

Dr. Lee is the author of sixteen books, including several bestsellers in Korea, and has also released two well-received musical CDs. He is a well-known lecturer on topics ranging from spiritual health to enlightenment, speaking in various locations including the Harvard School of Theology and Queens College of New York City. In 2000, he and Neale Donald Walsch, the well-known author of the *Conversations with God* series, established the New Millennium Peace Foundation, a non-profit foundation whose goal is to attain a lasting world peace by raising the collective human awareness. Dr. Lee and Neale Donald Walsch lecture at "The Meeting with the Creator," an event held several times a year in Sedona, Arizona, and other locations around the world.

Dr. Lee was recognized as one of the fifty preeminent spiritual leaders of the world at the recent United Nations

World Peace Summit of Religious and Spiritual Leaders (August 2000), attended by some 1,000 of the world's religious and spiritual leaders. At that event, he announced the continuation of the World Peace Summit in Korea in June 2001, declared his intentions to establish a "Peace Park" in the Demilitarized Zone between South and North Korea, and his plans to establish a Spiritual U.N. in Sedona, Arizona.

Healing Society not only contains the essence of the enlightenment that Dr. Seung Heun Lee has personally experienced but also presents an outline of the efforts we, as individuals, need to begin making to open up a new era of worldwide spiritual awakening. Due to the large number of inquiries into *Dahn Hak* and Brain Respiration, the mind and body training methods espoused in the book, Dr. Lee plans to publish an English language instructional training manual in the near future.

For further information on *Dahn Hak* and Brain Respiration and for locations of Healing Society study groups, visit the Internet site at www.healingsociety.com, or call 1-877-DAHNHAK, toll free.

WALSCH

BOOKS

Visions of the Spirit

Walsch Books is an imprint of Hampton Roads Publishing Company,
edited by Neale Donald Walsch and Nancy Fleming-Walsch.
Our shared vision is to publish quality books that enhance and
further the central messages of the Conversations with God series,
in both fiction and non-fiction genres, and to provide another a
venue through which the healing truths of the great wisdom
traditions may be expressed in clear and accessible terms.

Hampton Roads Publishing Company

... for the evolving human spirit

Hampton Roads Publishing Company
publishes books on a variety of subjects,
including metaphysics, health, integrative medicine,
visionary fiction, and other related topics.

For a copy of our latest catalog, call toll-free
(800) 766-8009, or send your name and address to:

Hampton Roads Publishing Company, Inc.
1125 Stoney Ridge Road
Charlottesville, VA 22902

e-mail: hrpc@hrpub.com
Website: www.hrpub.com